GLAMOUR

MODEL REVUE

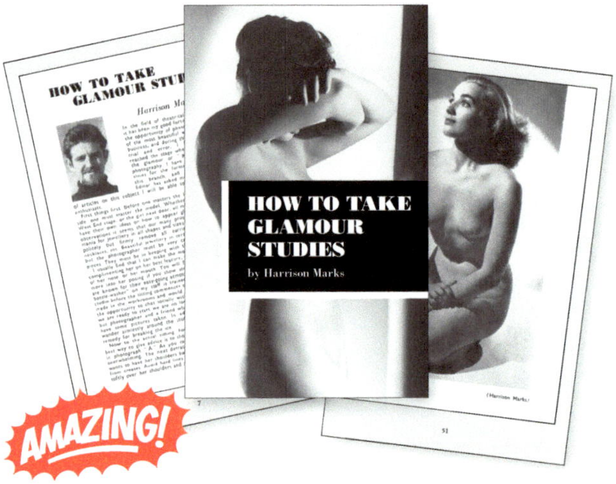

Published in 2023 by Wolfbait Books
www.wolfbait.co.uk

ISBN: 9781916215191

A catalogue record of this book is available at the British Library.

Below: Paula Page.

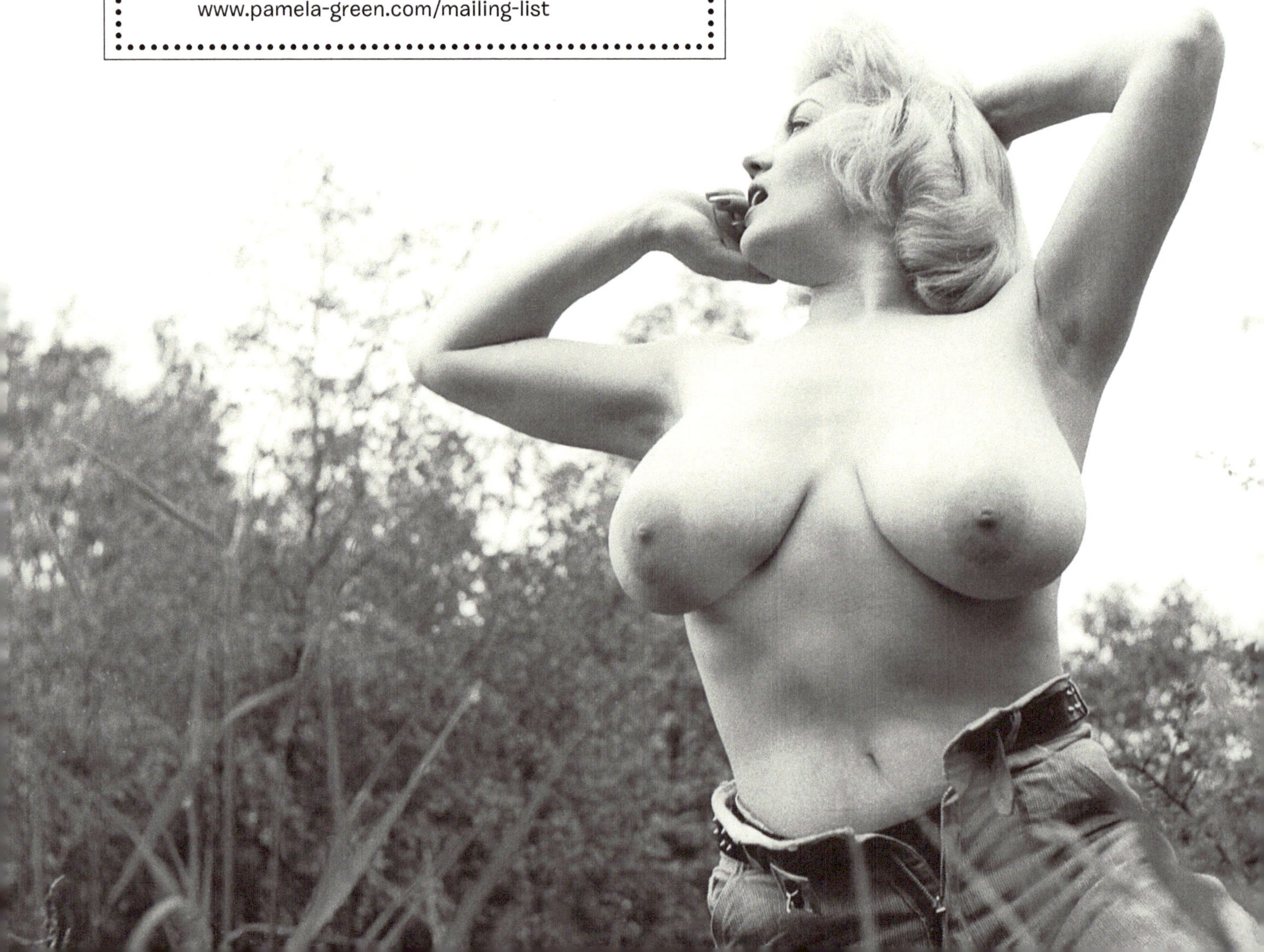

GLAMOUR

MODEL REVUE

FEATURING

JUNE PALMER ★ PAULA PAGE ★ TINA MADISON

By Yahya El-Droubie

Photography by Eva Grant

WOLFBAIT

UNDER THE COUNTER CULTURE

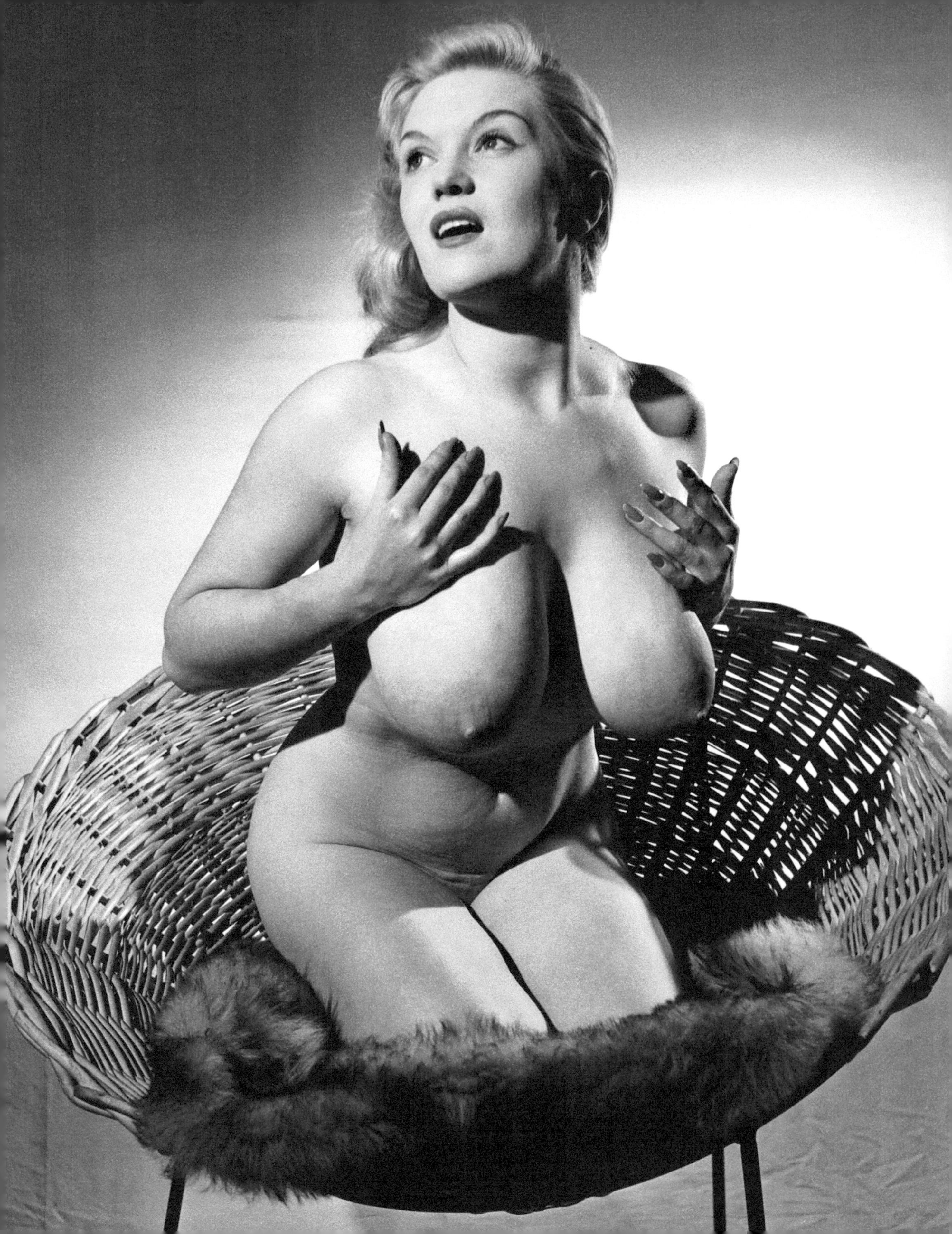

Framing Beauty

IT WAS ONCE SAID that a female model can only give her best when posing for a male photographer. That there needs to be a little sexual chemistry between the pair in order to capture that elusive *je ne sais quoi*. However, the pioneering images taken by one talented, self-taught woman photographer proved that this isn't always the case. Eva Grant, hailing from Greece but considering herself a Londoner, was once described as "the world's leading female camera artist". During her successful career in the late 1950s and early 1960s, she worked and thrived in the male-dominated field of glamour photography, her beautifully lit nude studies gracing the pages of publications on both sides of the Atlantic.

How can I tell whether a girl with her clothes on will make a good model? Well, the face has to be just right. As to the rest of the body, that is strictly a hunch; a hunch and a reasonable knowledge of female anatomy — though sometimes I'm quite wrong.

— Eva Grant

In the glamour photography industry of the mid-20th century, an aspiring pin-up star had to do more than simply be willing to part with some of her clothes, while the possession of a pretty face and a fetching shape did not necessarily make a woman a good model. For the photographer, one of the main difficulties in creating successful glamour images was finding models with the right attributes and attitude. In the 1950s, unless a photographer changed locations frequently or lived in a large town, they would quickly exhaust the list of potential subjects among their acquaintances and friends, as well as the acquaintances of acquaintances. Eventually, they would find themselves presenting magazine editors with images of the same old faces rather than fresh new ones.

In London, there were two ways that a glamour photographer could find models to shoot. The first was to do the rounds of the model agencies, so that as soon as a new face appeared on the scene, they could pounce and snap them up before other talent-searching photographers discovered them. However, a better approach was to haunt the coffee bars and jiving cellars where young people congregated and keep one's eyes skinned for likely prospects.

As a woman, Eva had an easier job finding newcomers than her male counterparts, as she could approach a girl with model potential with much less awkwardness.

Opposite: Paula Page, affectionately known as 'Two Guns Paula', 1958.

Just looking for a beautiful shape would bore me. I'm always looking for a mood – gay, serious, pensive, whimsical...
— Eva Grant

She found that most girls were thrilled about having their photographs published in a magazine. Back then, as is still the case today, figure models came in all shapes and sizes, from boyish to kittenish to Rubenesque. The three professional models featured in this volume are prime examples of this wide variety.

June Palmer was the most famous of the Harrison Marks glamour models of the 1960s and arguably the most celebrated British figure model of all time. Born in Bromley, Kent, her modelling career spanned two decades, and along with her partner, Arthur Howell, she ran a model agency and photography studio above a camera shop in Clapham, London, from the 1950s until the late 1980s.

Paula Page's modelling career began in the late 1950s. Born in Shropshire in the late 1930s, she studied to be a typist, but took to nude modelling when she realised how much attention her 44DD-23-36 figure was attracting. She went on to become one of the most celebrated big-breasted British models of the era.

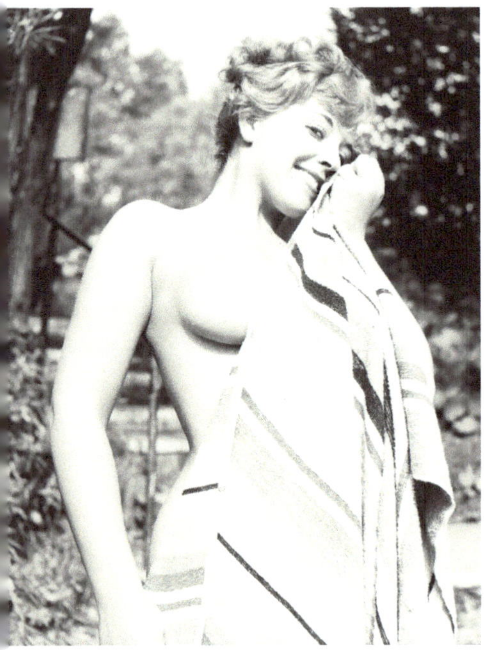

Above: Tina Madison at the Thames Sun Club, the premises of which consists of a little island near Sunbury-on-Thames.

Tina Madison was another regular model on the circuit, working for such photographers as Harrison Marks and Russell Gay, as well as Eva Grant. She appeared in numerous magazines, including *Kamera, Model* and *QT*. All three models starred in several 8mm striptease films.

For an overview of Eva Grant's life and photography career, see our companion publication *The Glamour Camera of Eva Grant* – in the meantime, enjoy the *Glamour Model Revue*.

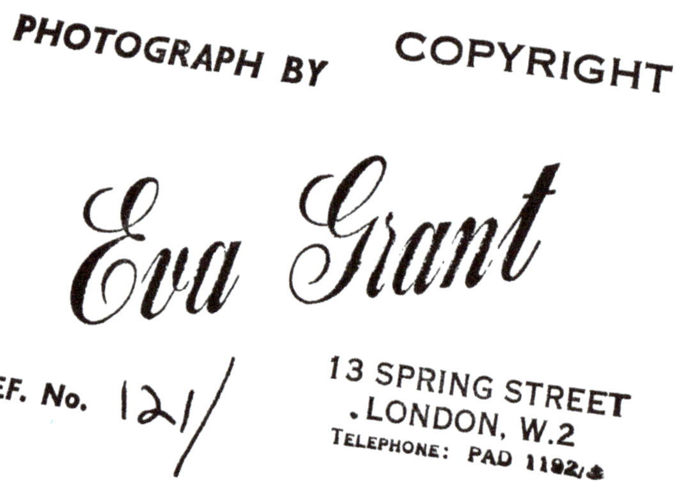

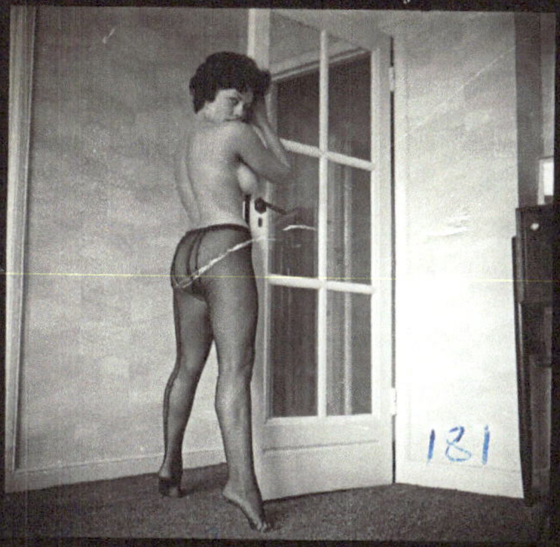

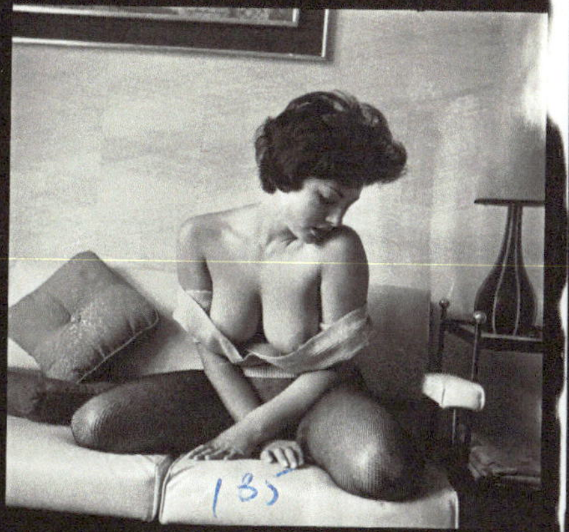

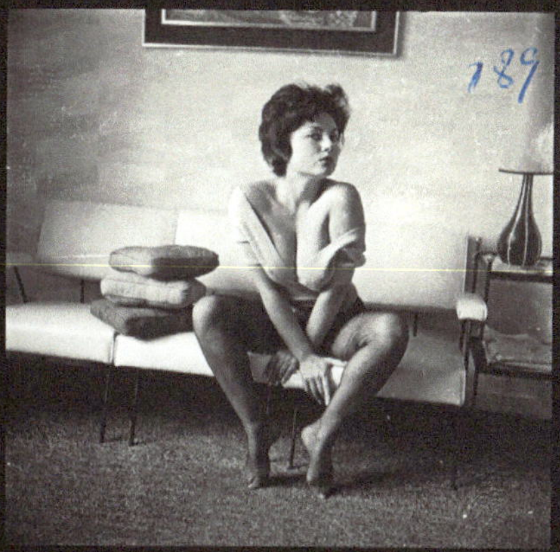

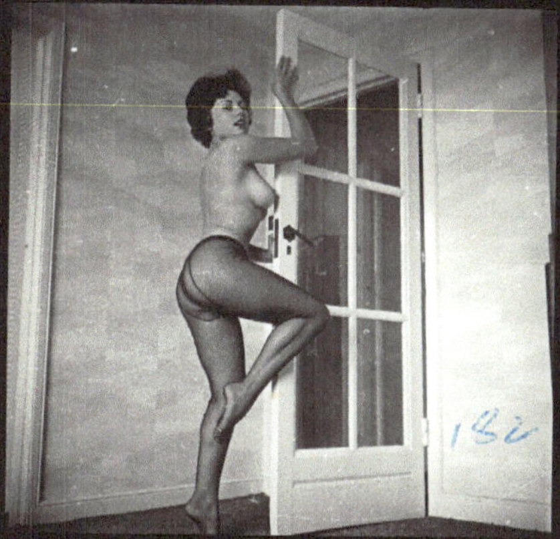

June Palmer

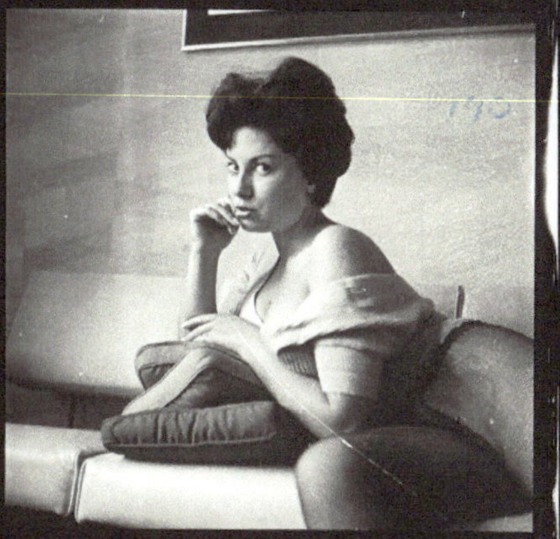
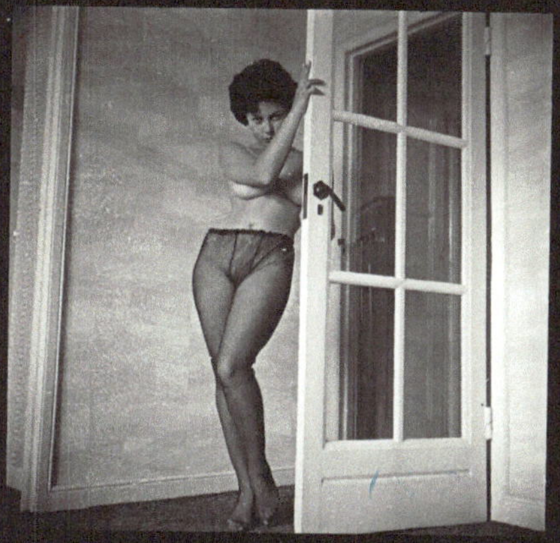
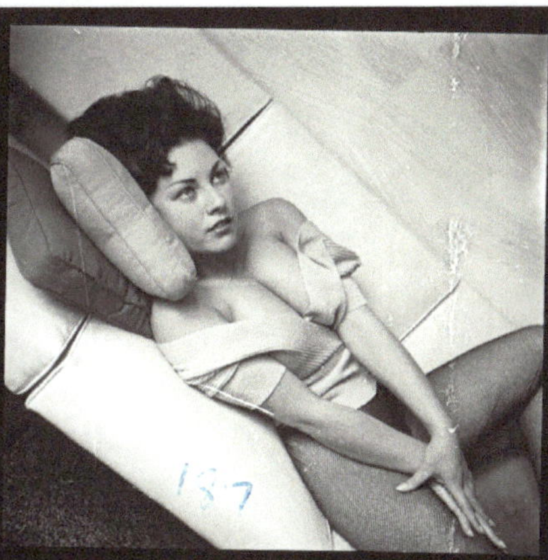

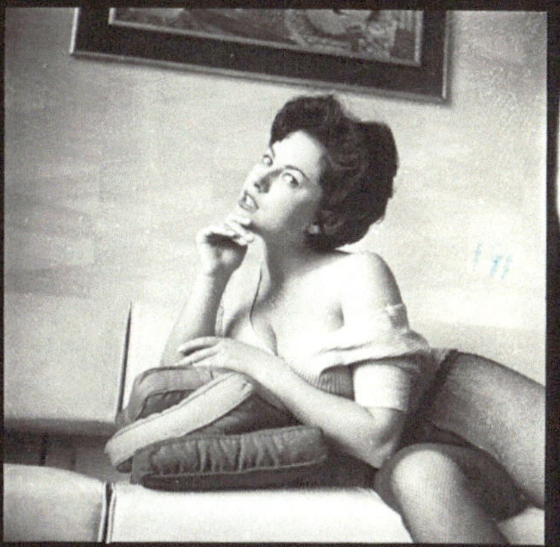
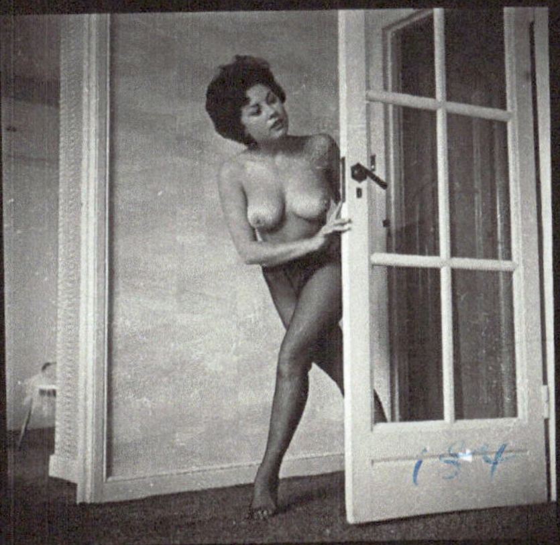

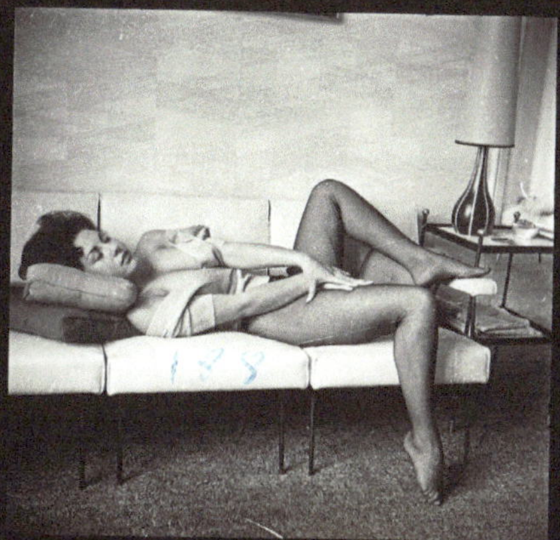

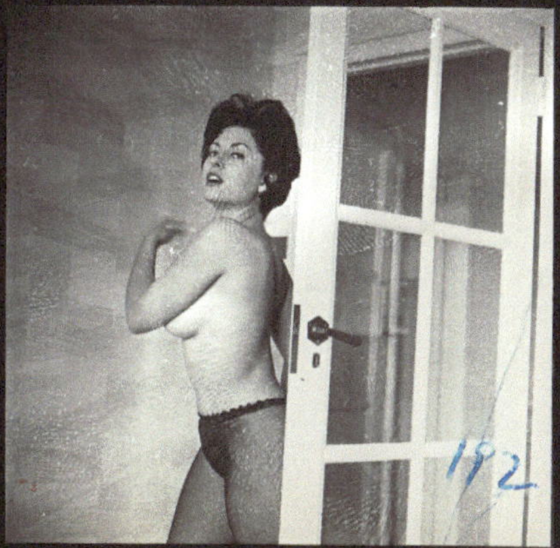

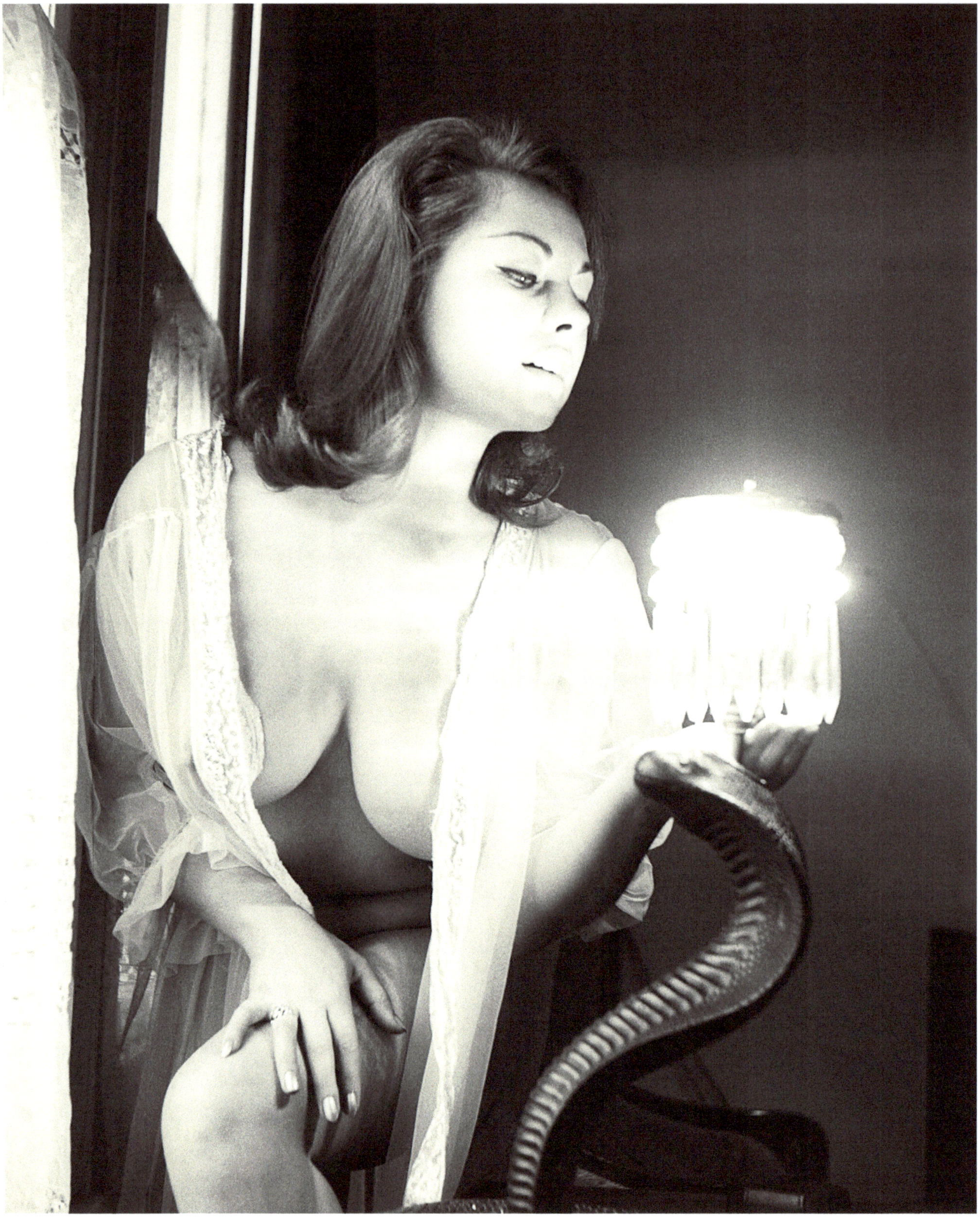

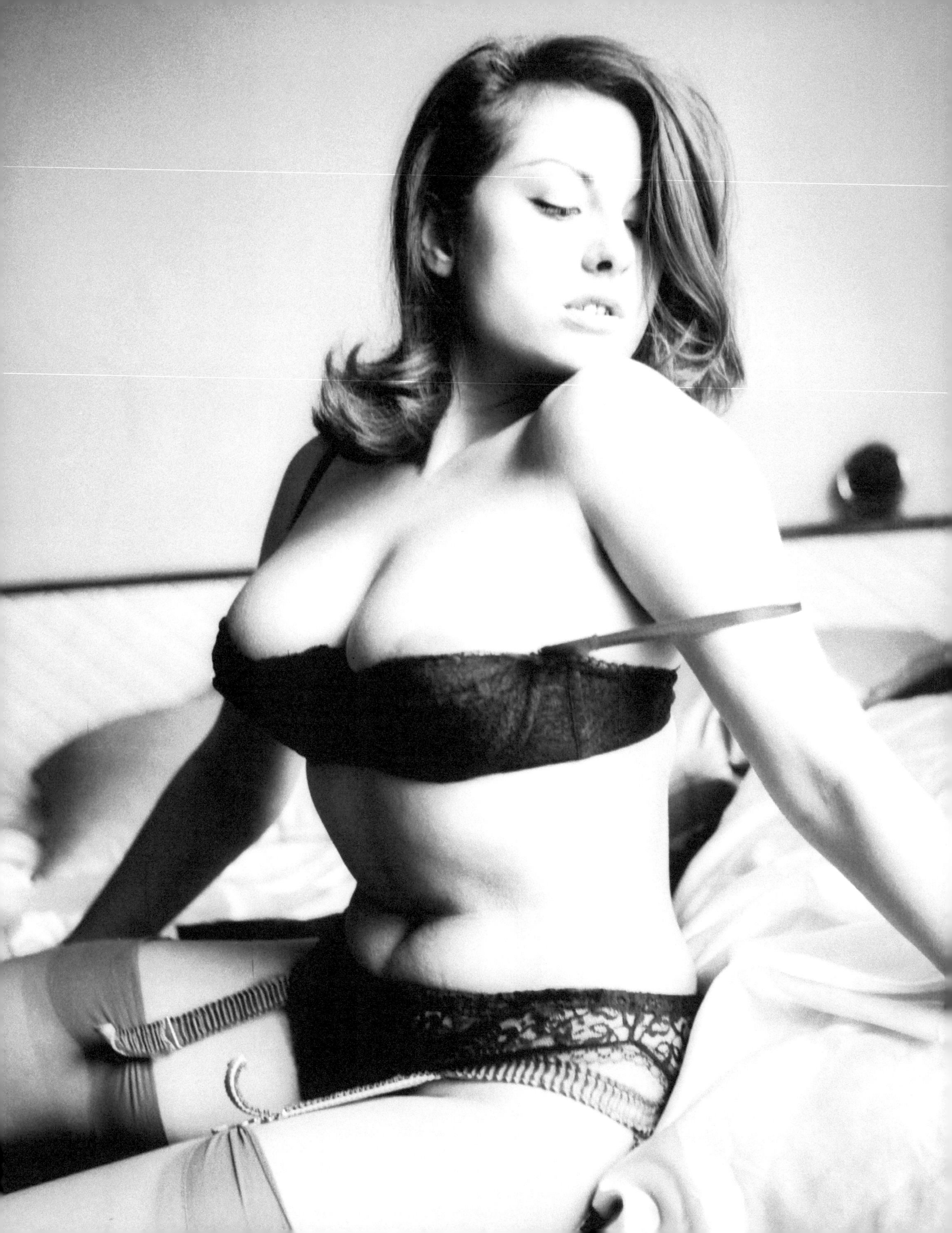

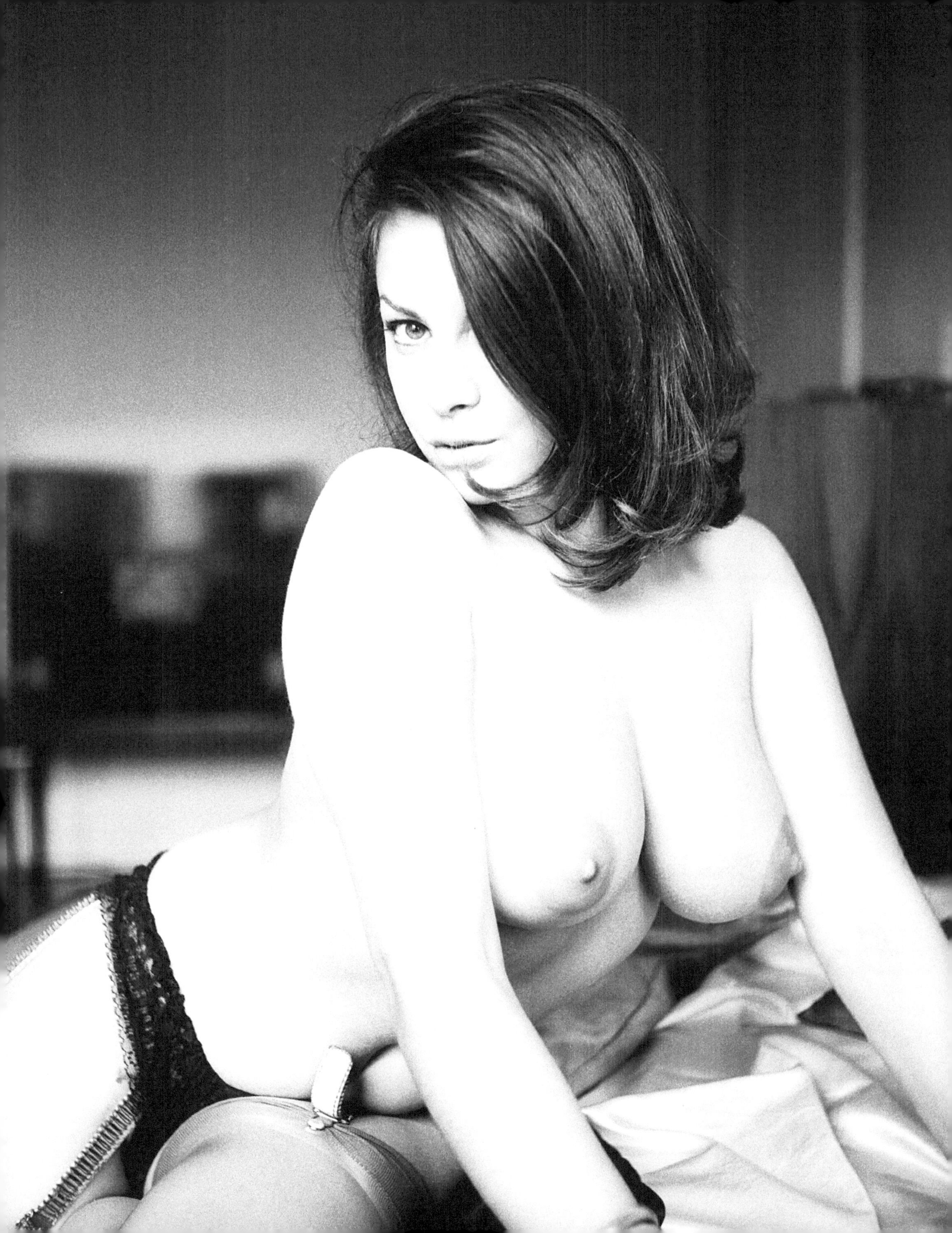

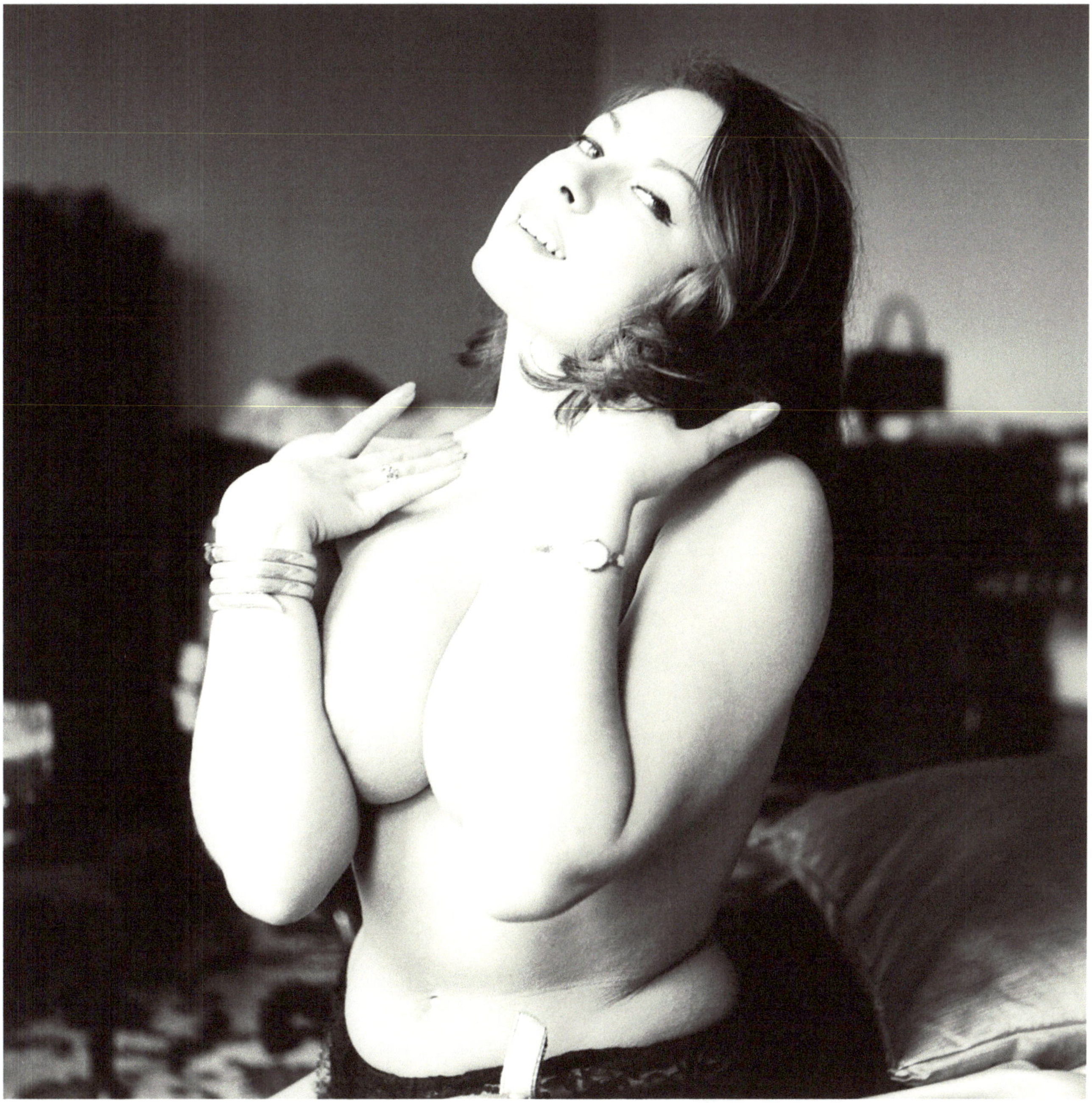

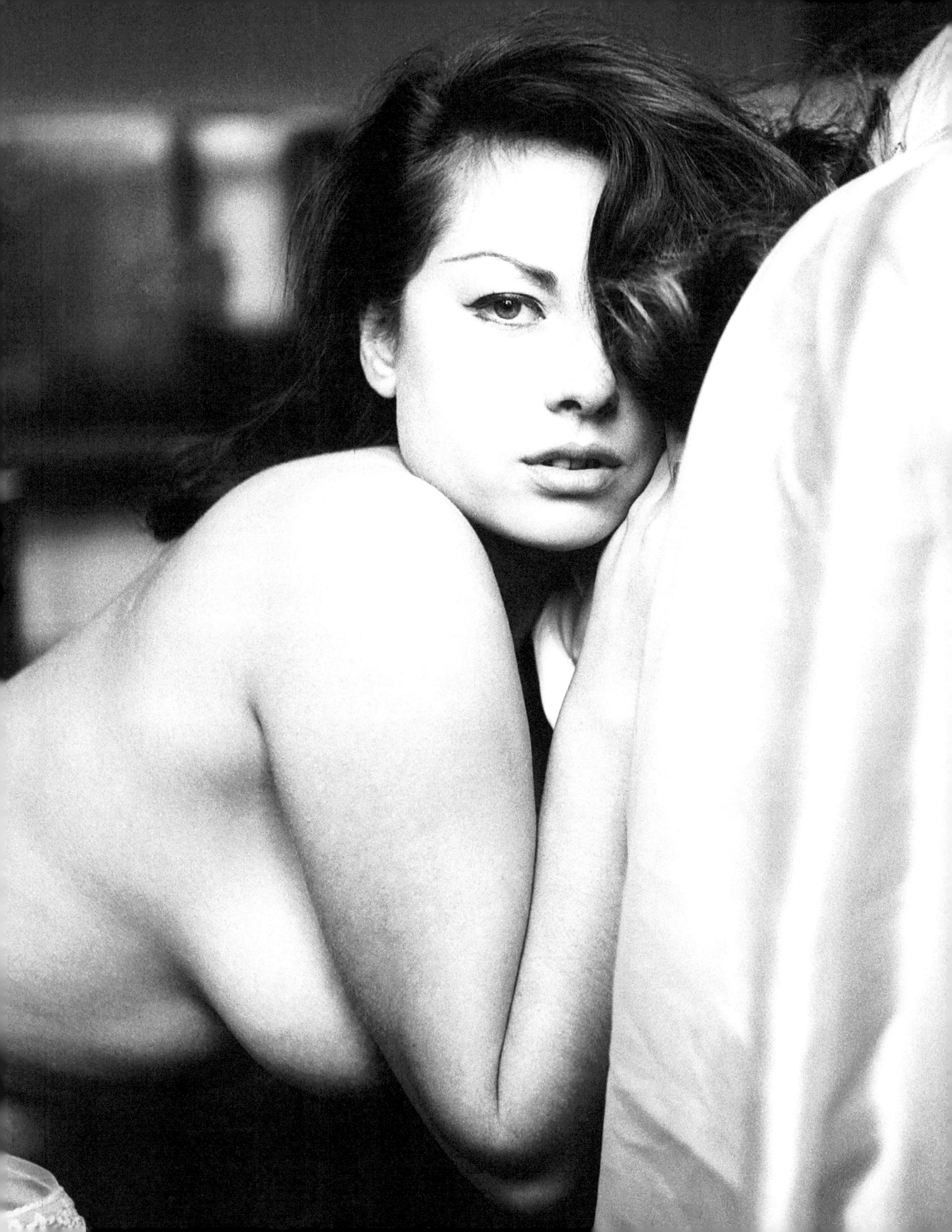

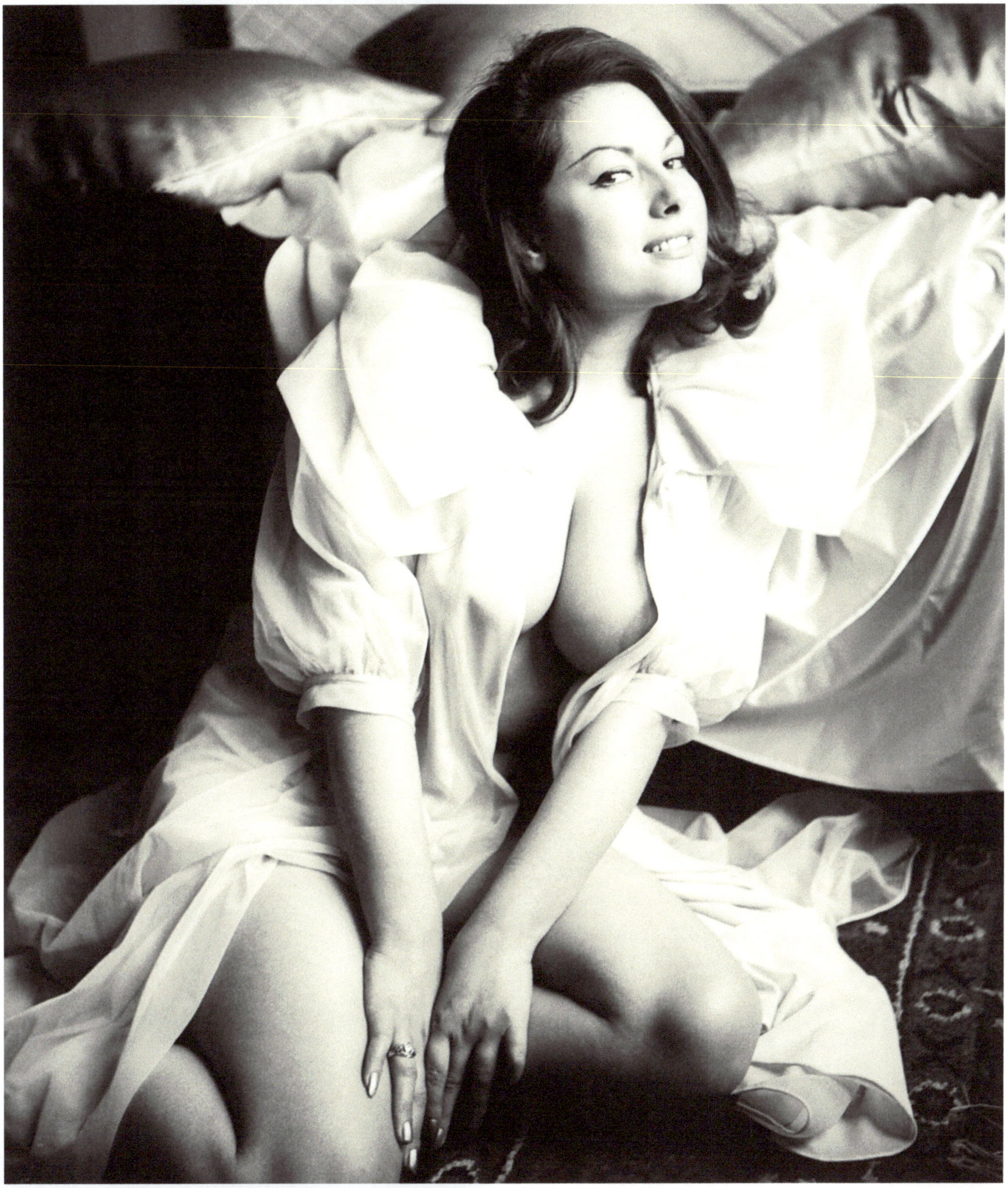

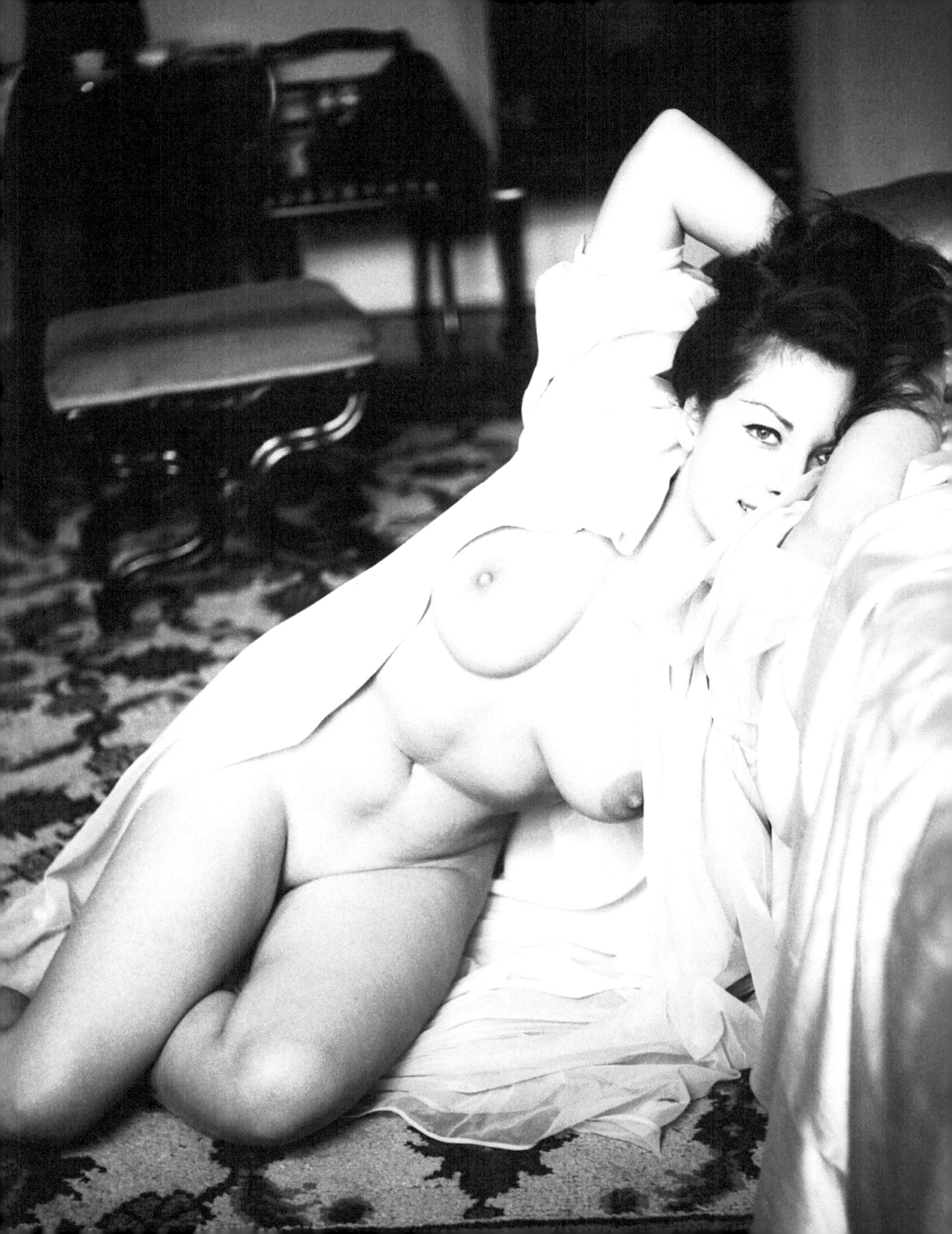

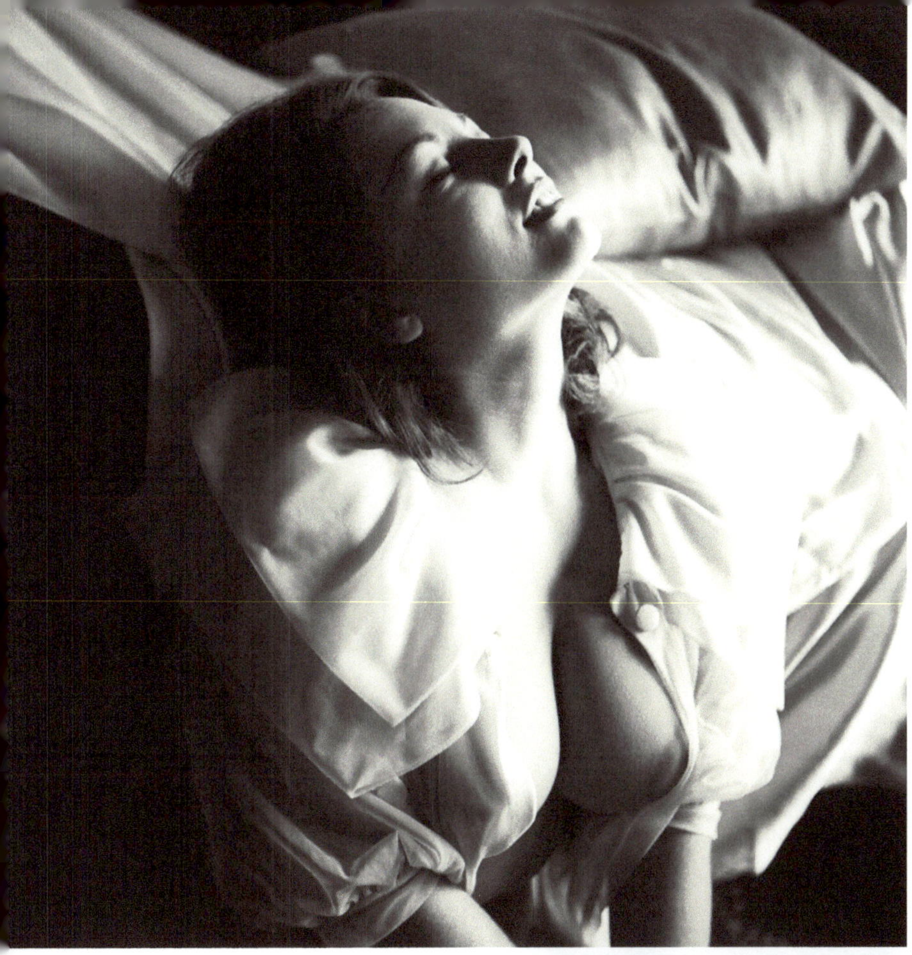

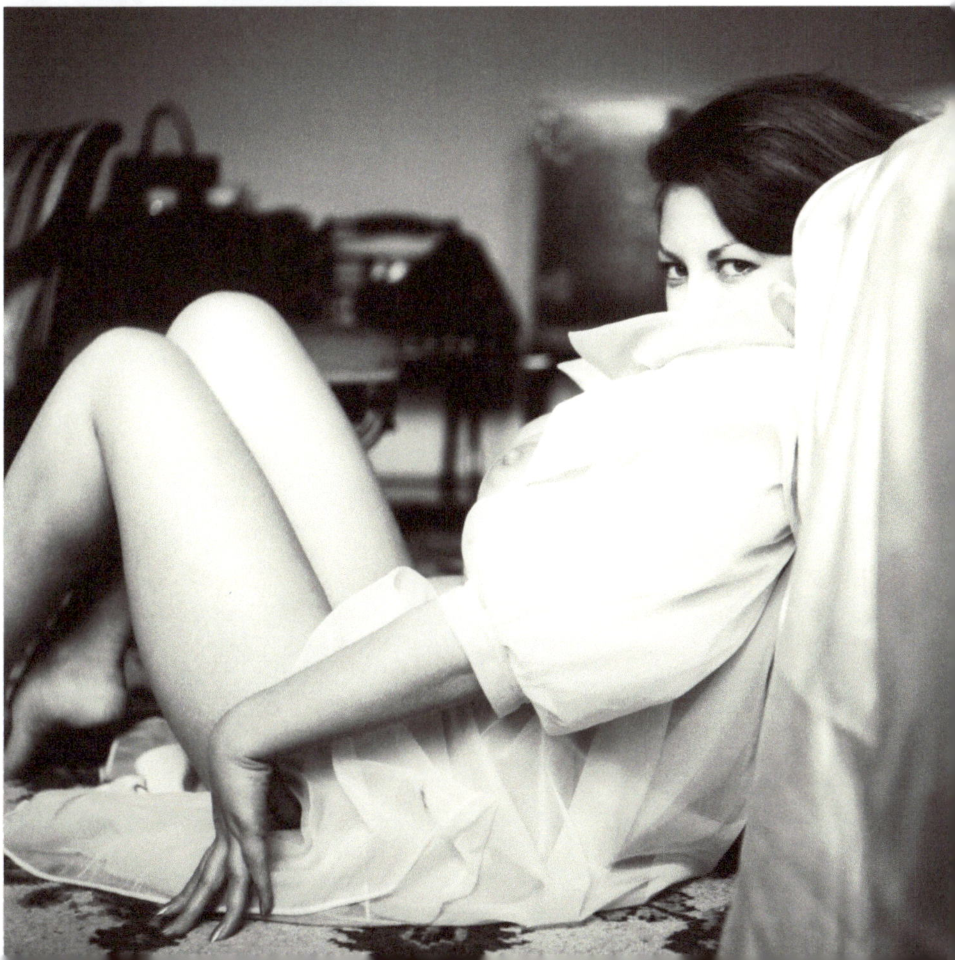

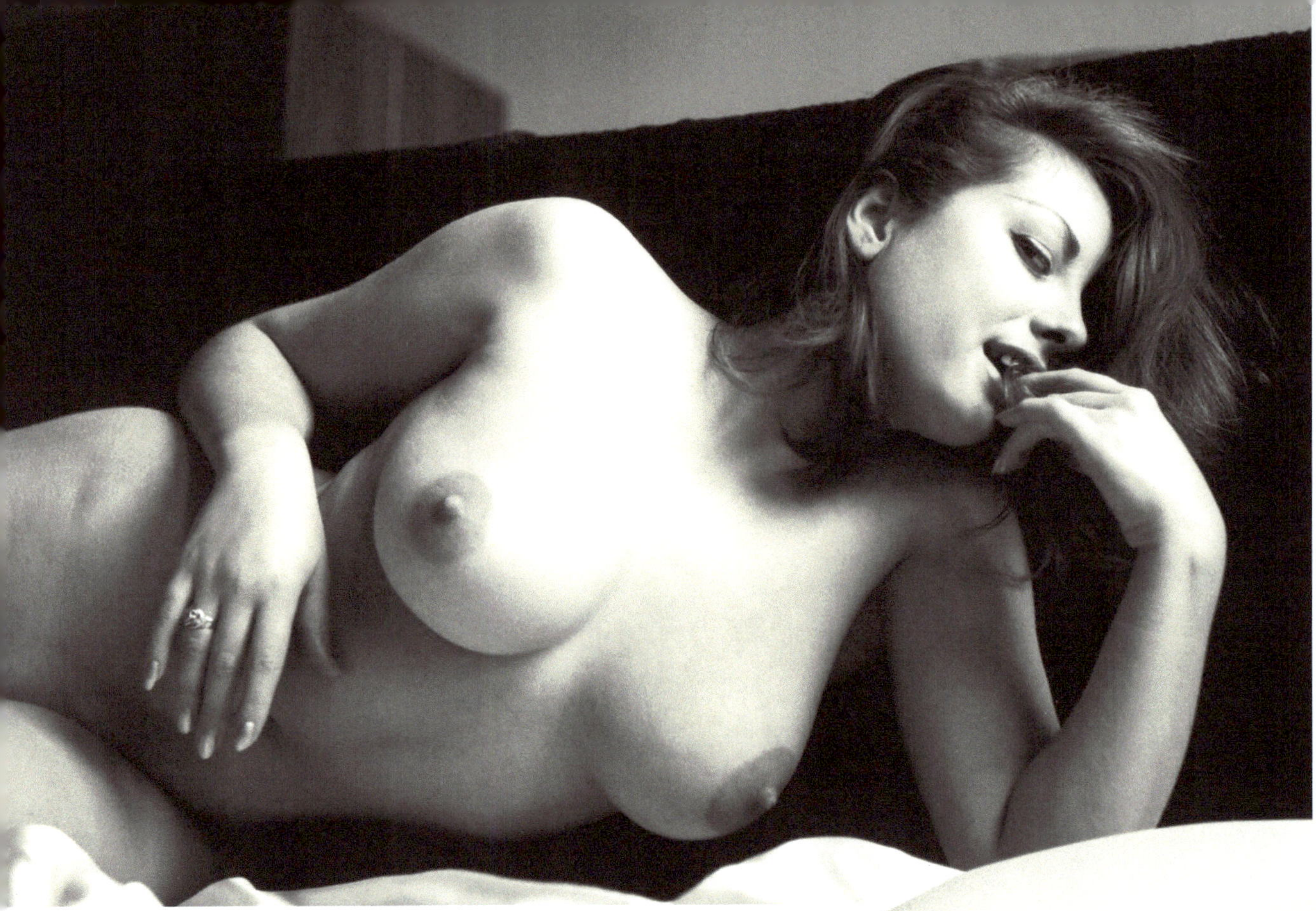

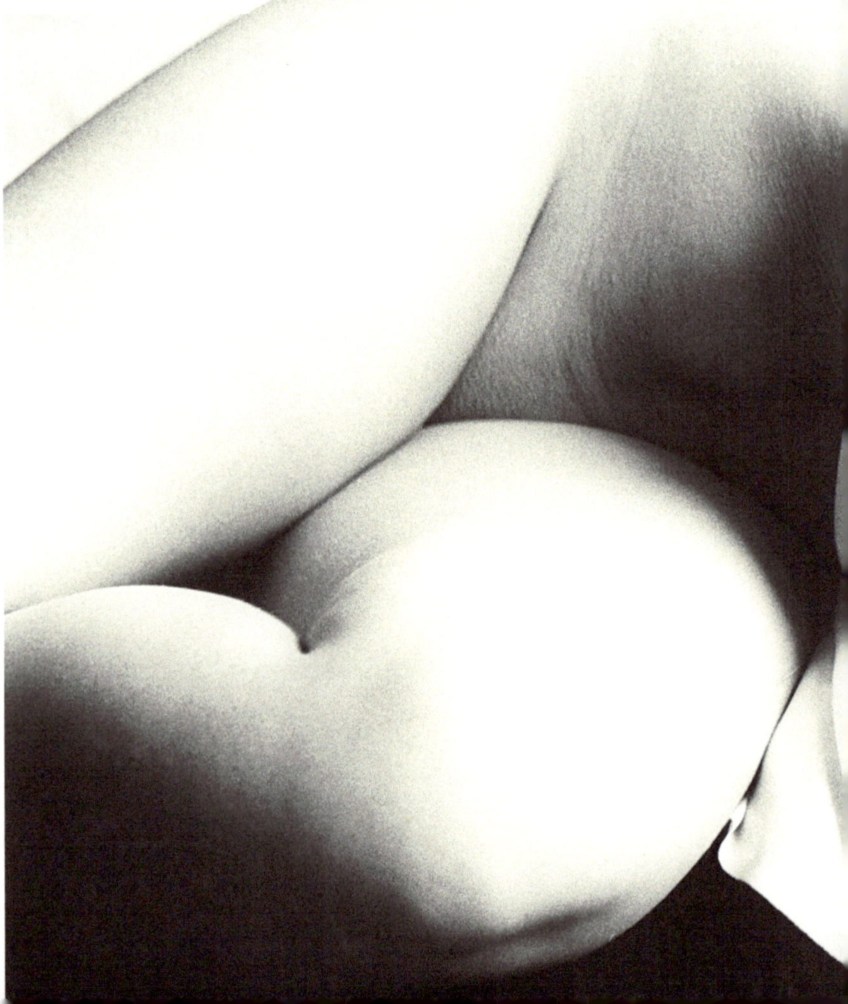

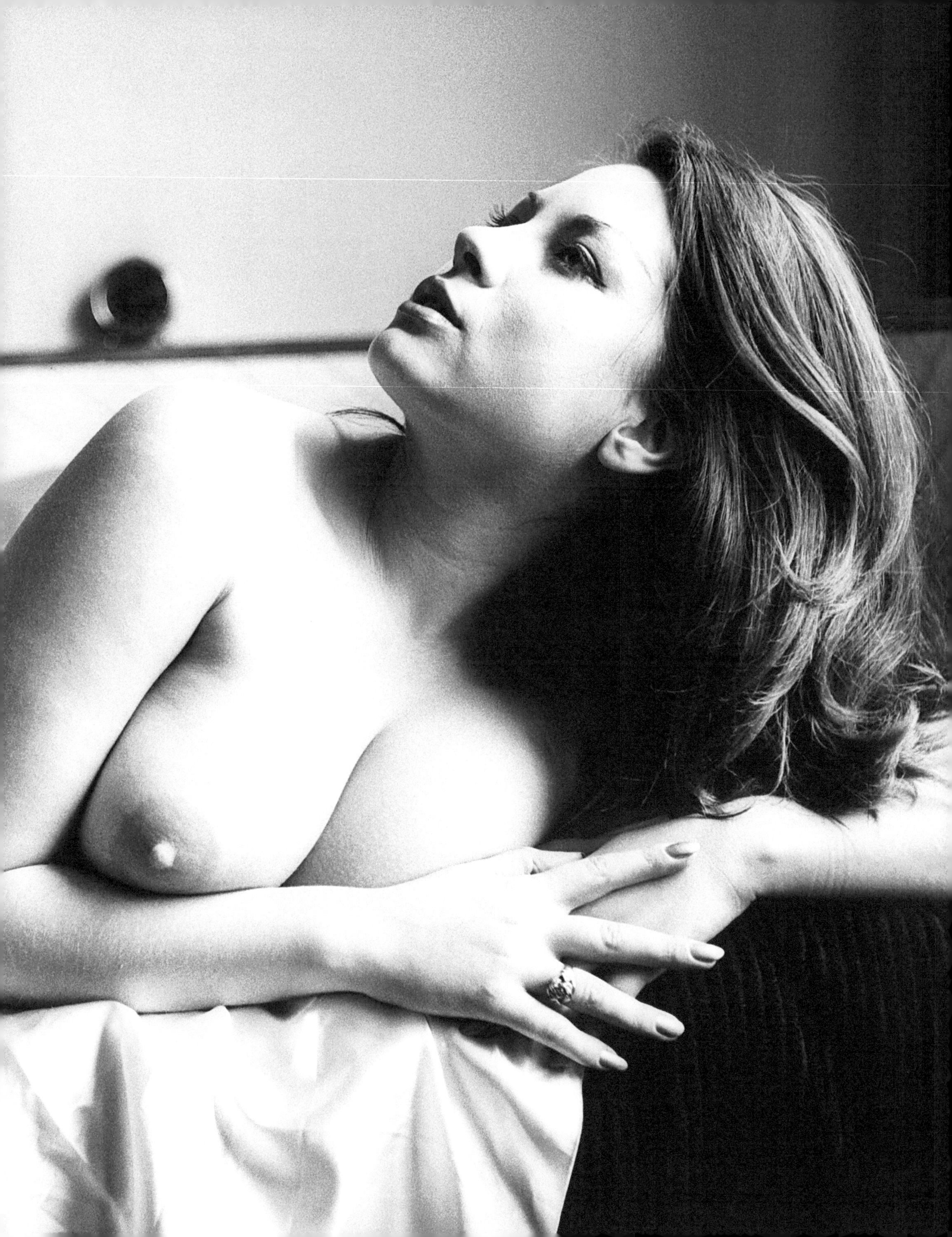

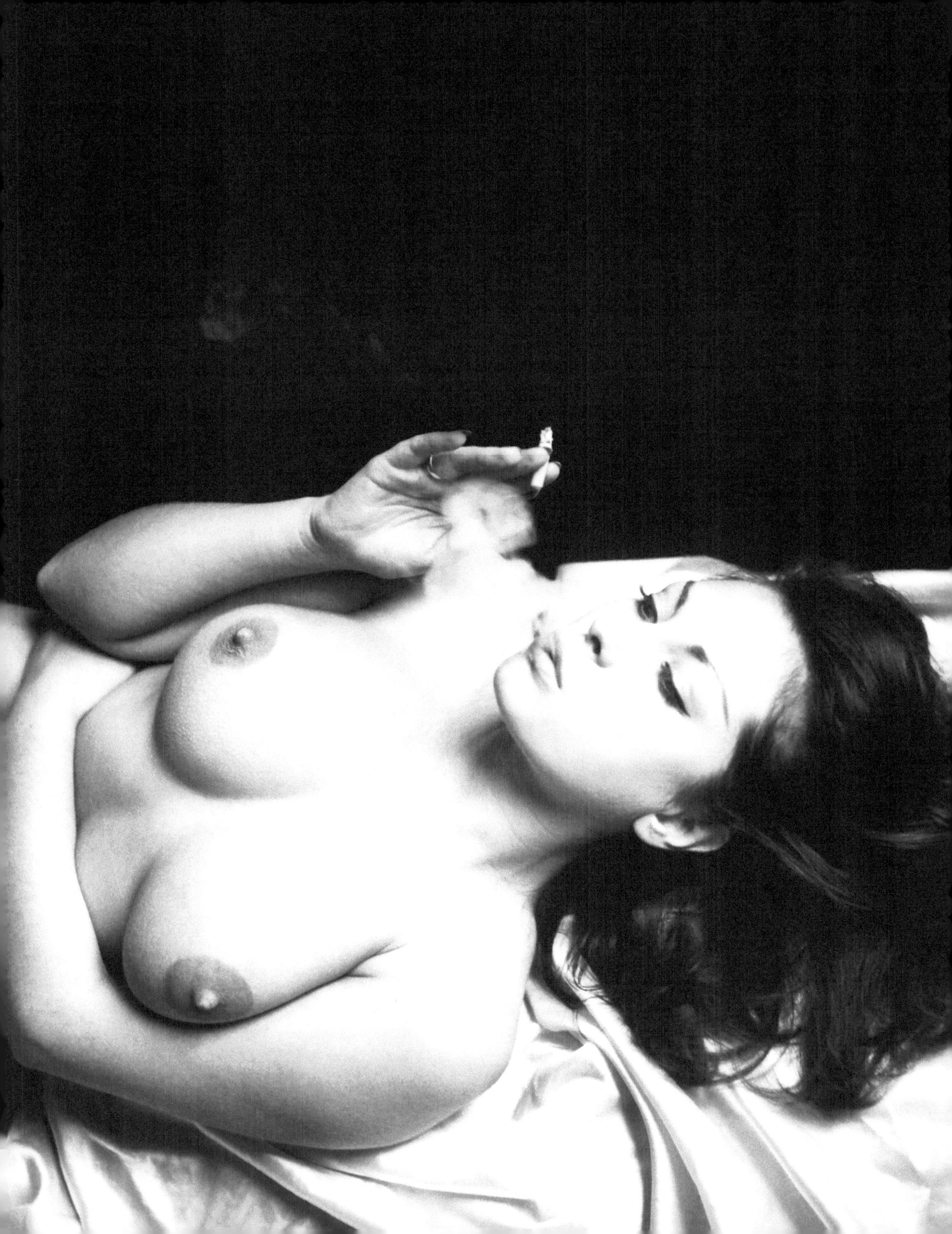

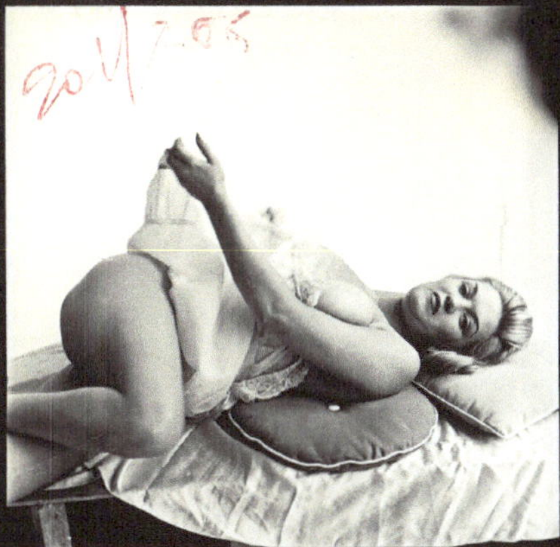

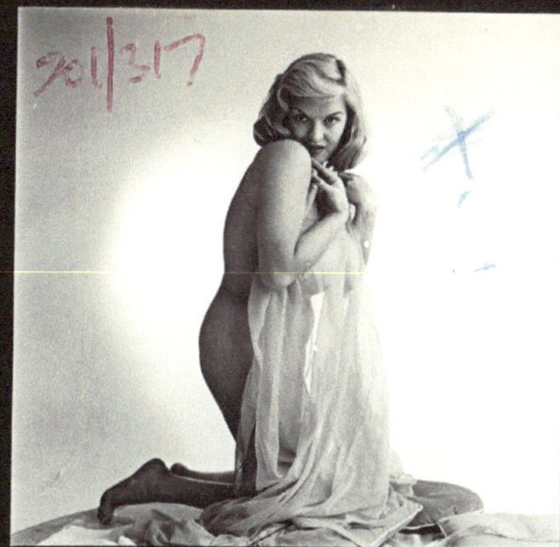

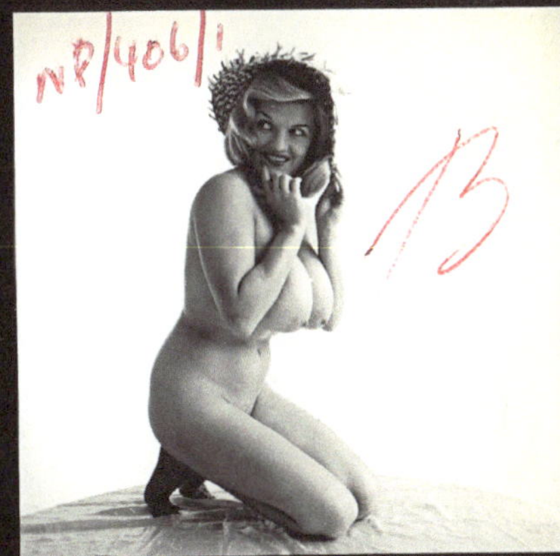

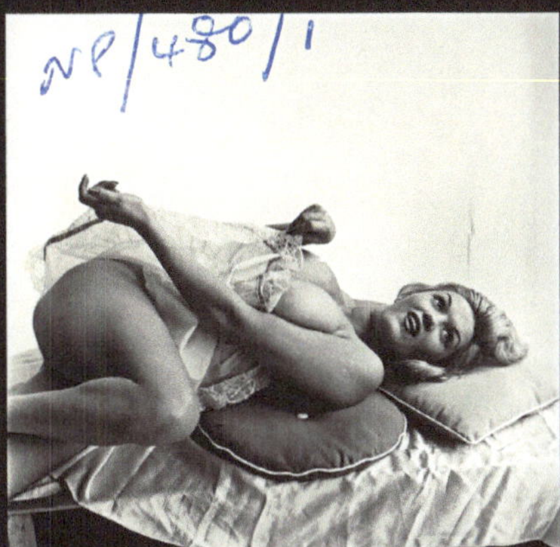

Paula Page

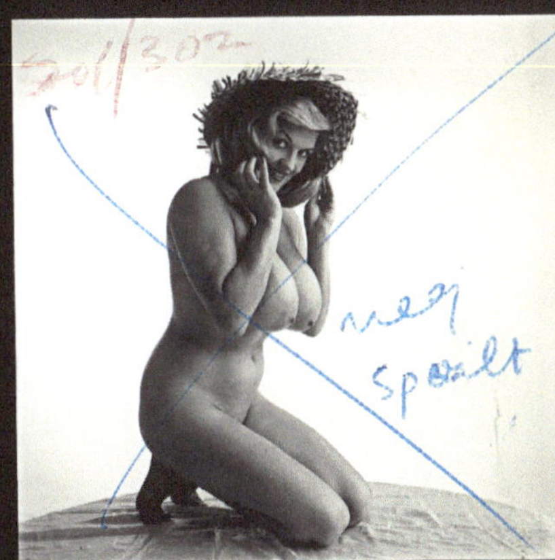

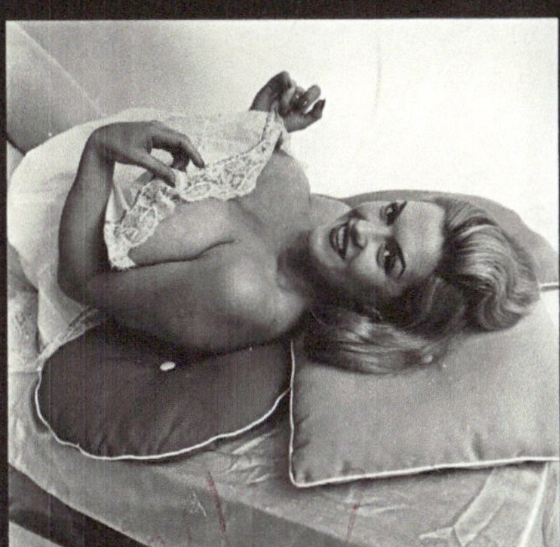

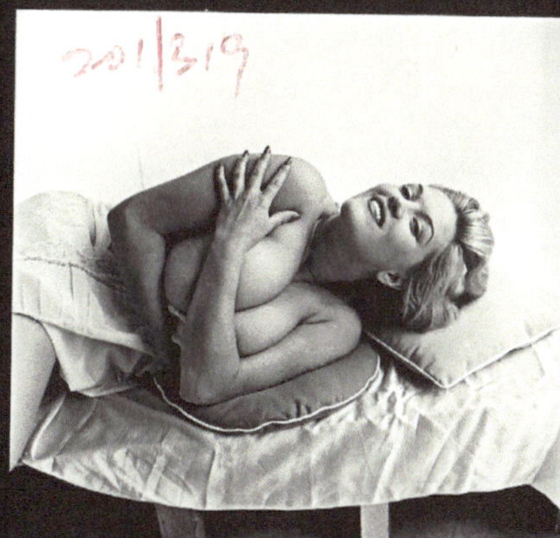

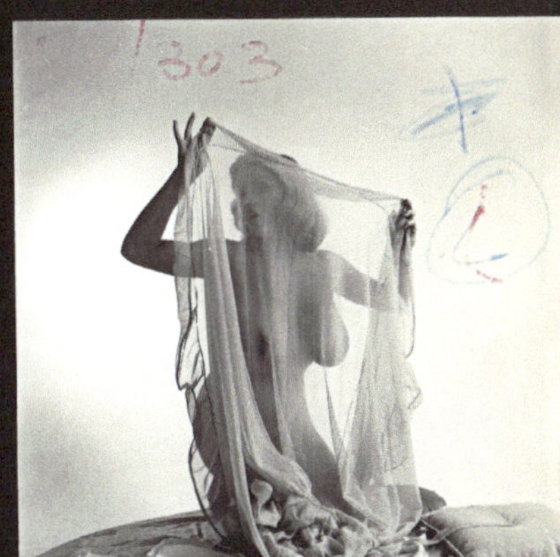

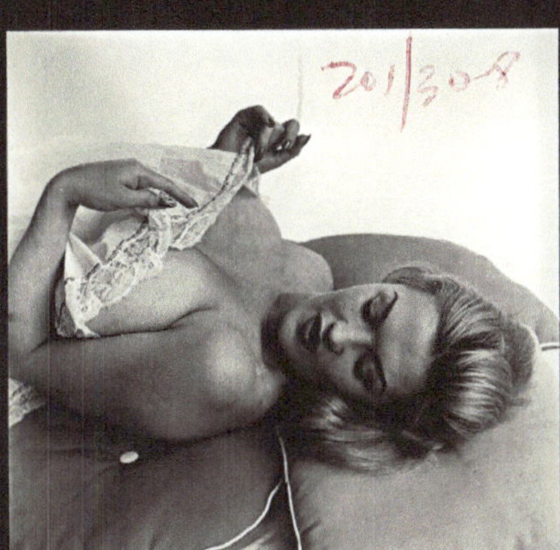

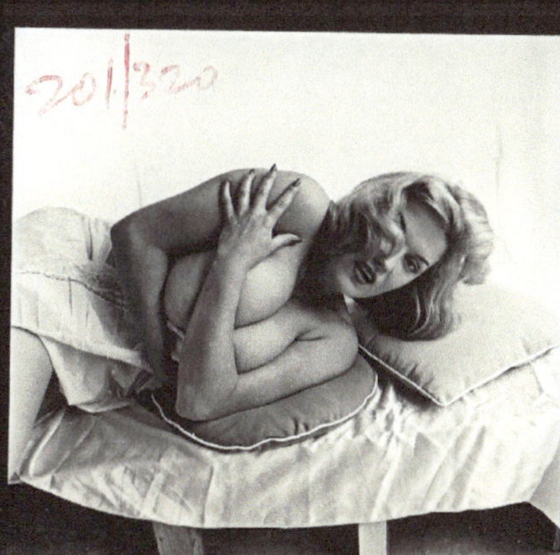

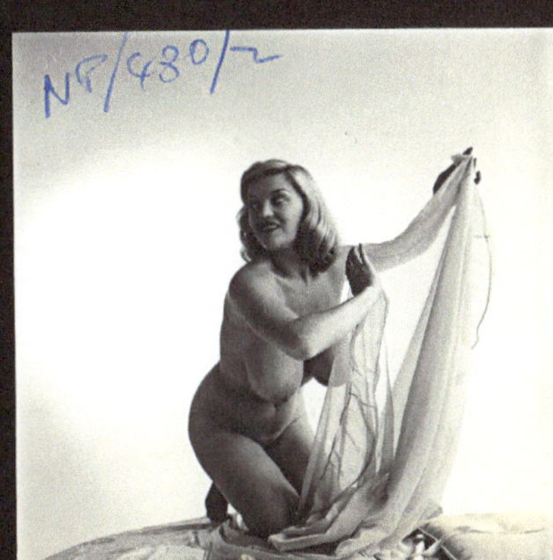

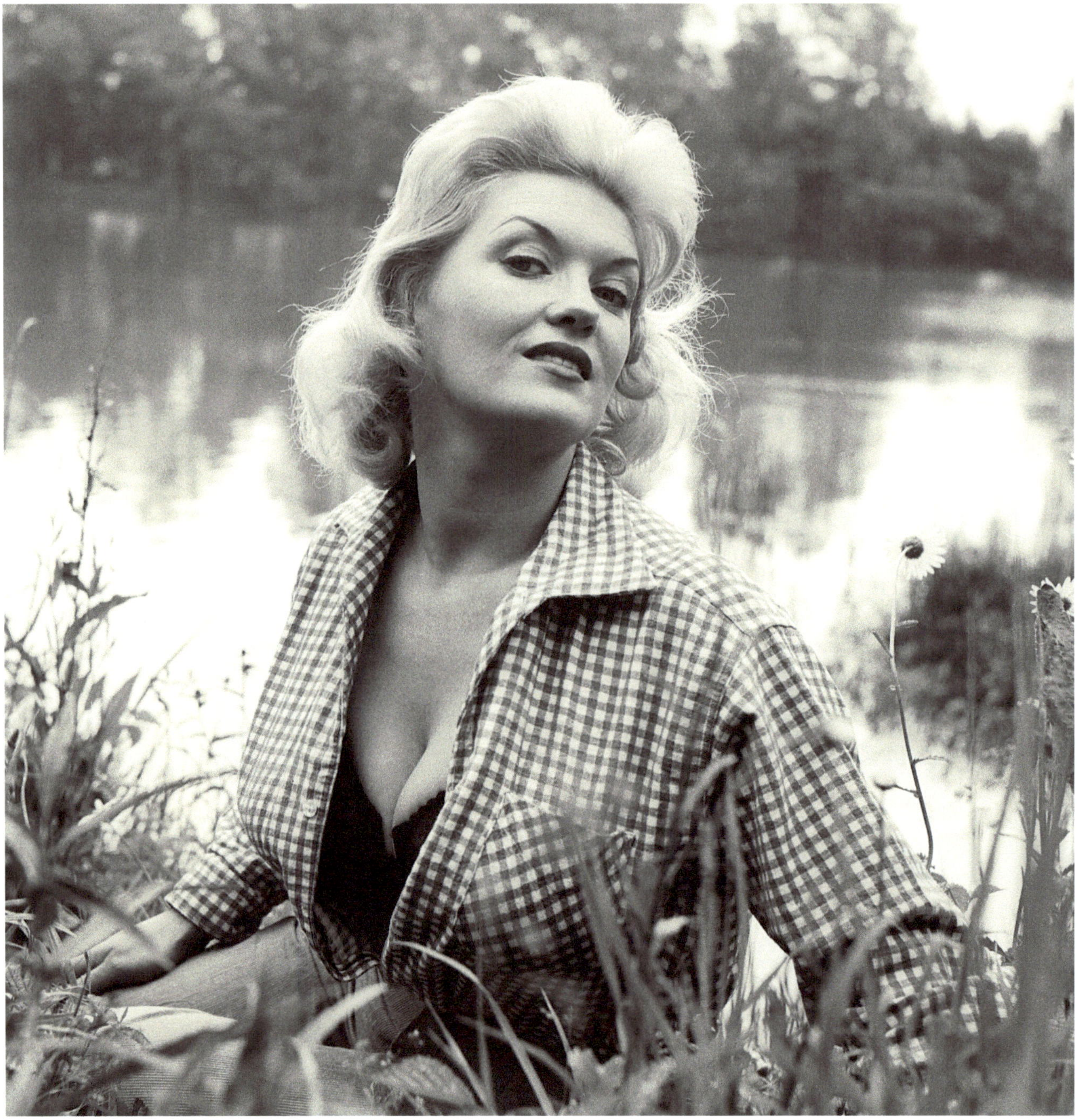

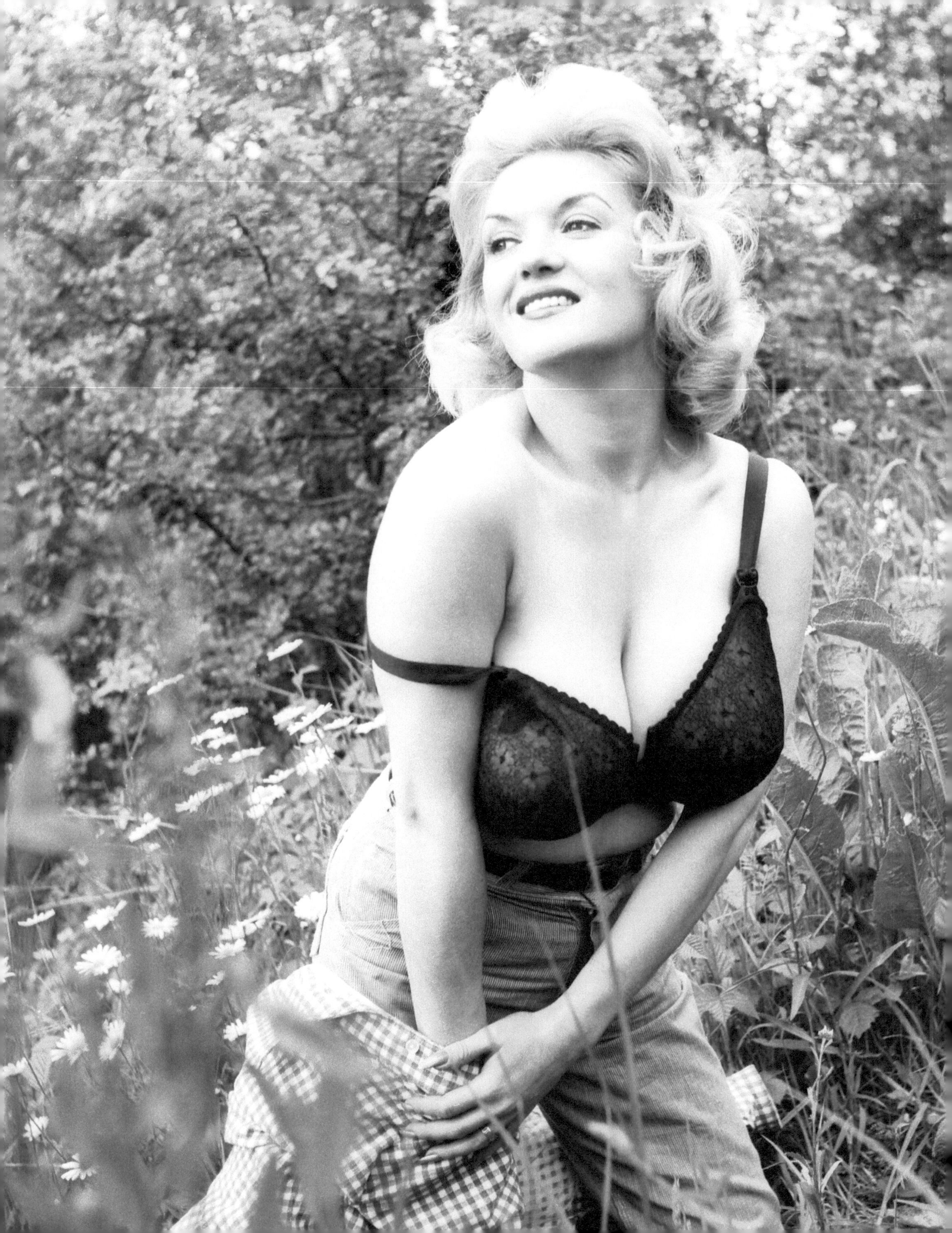

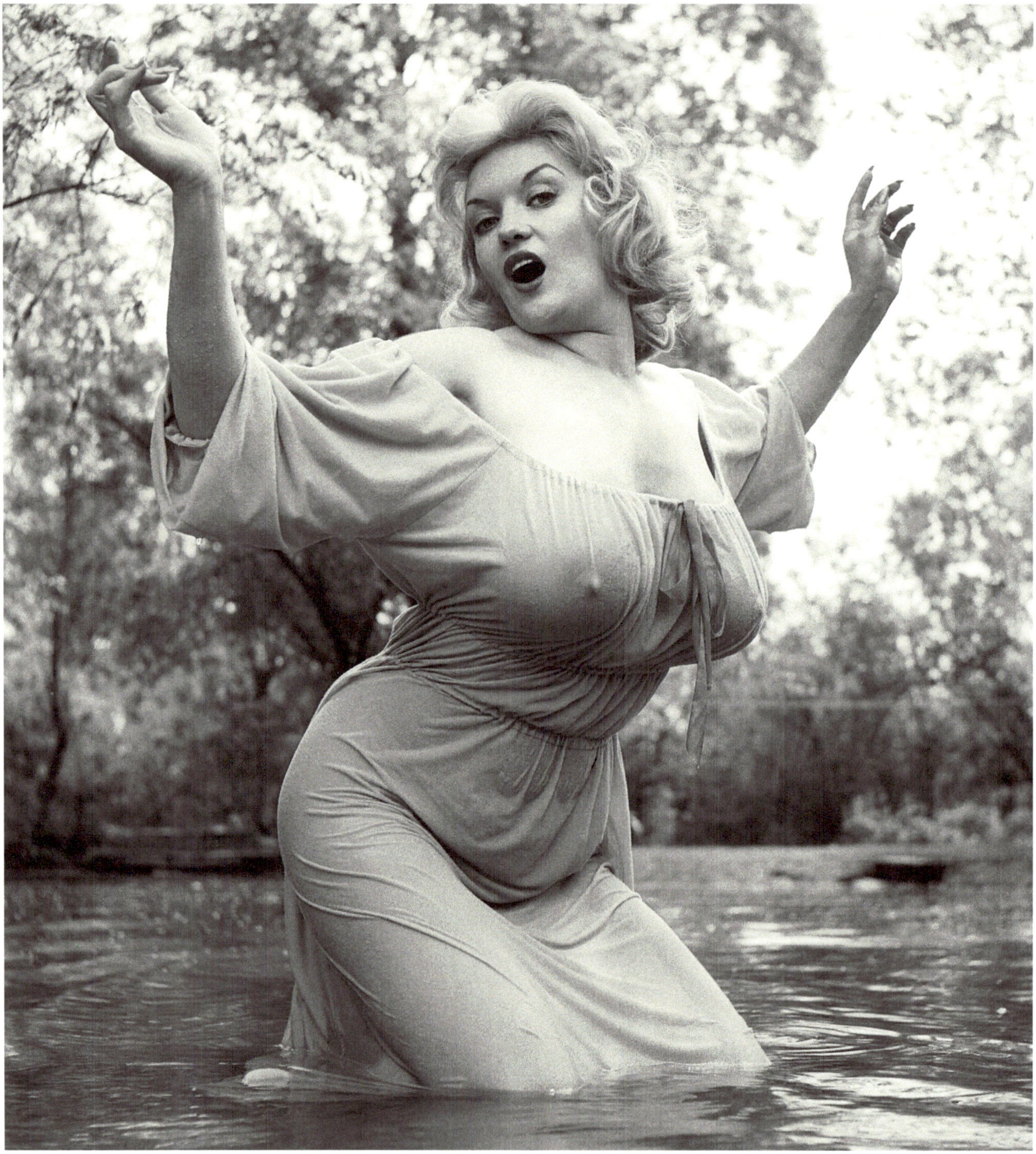

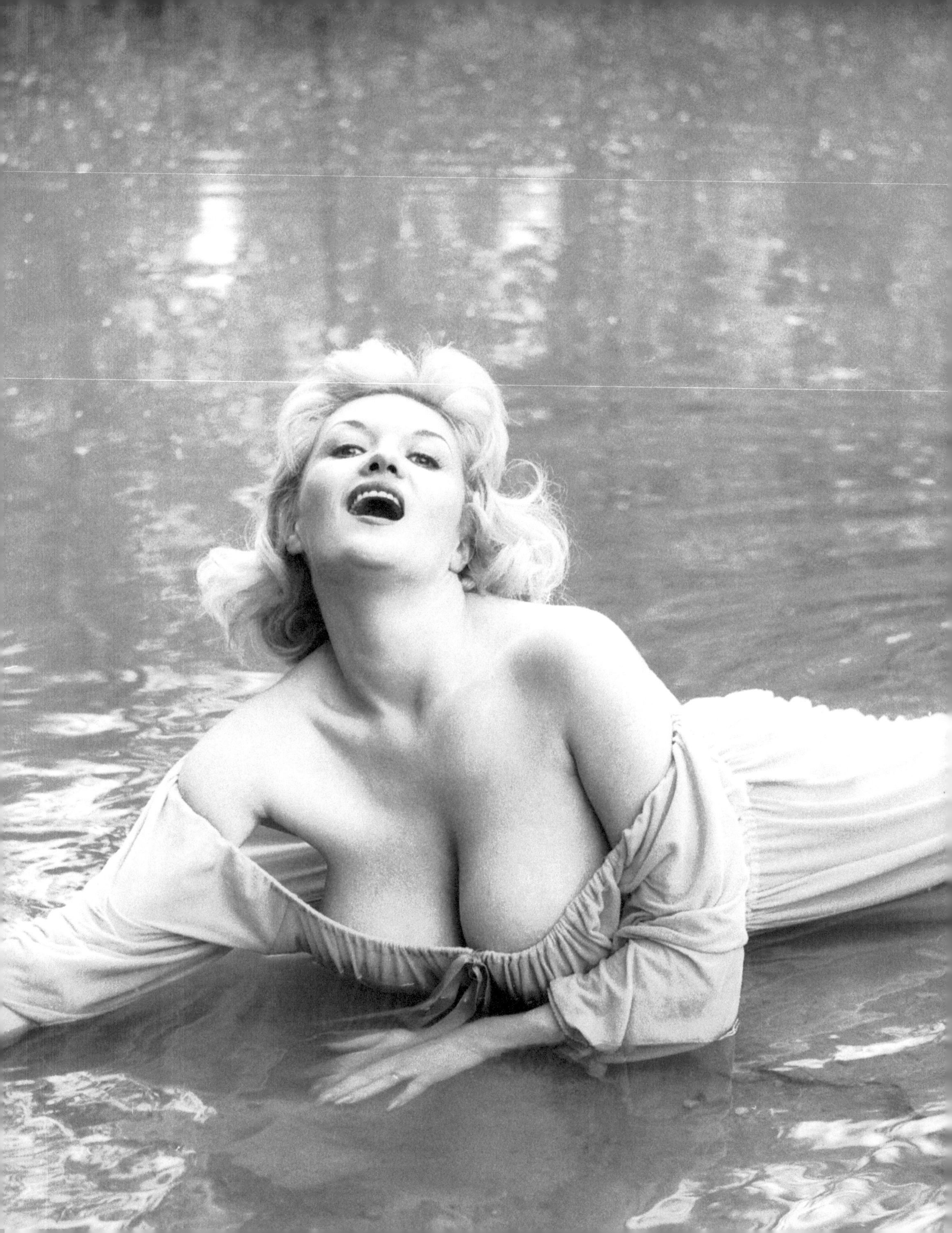

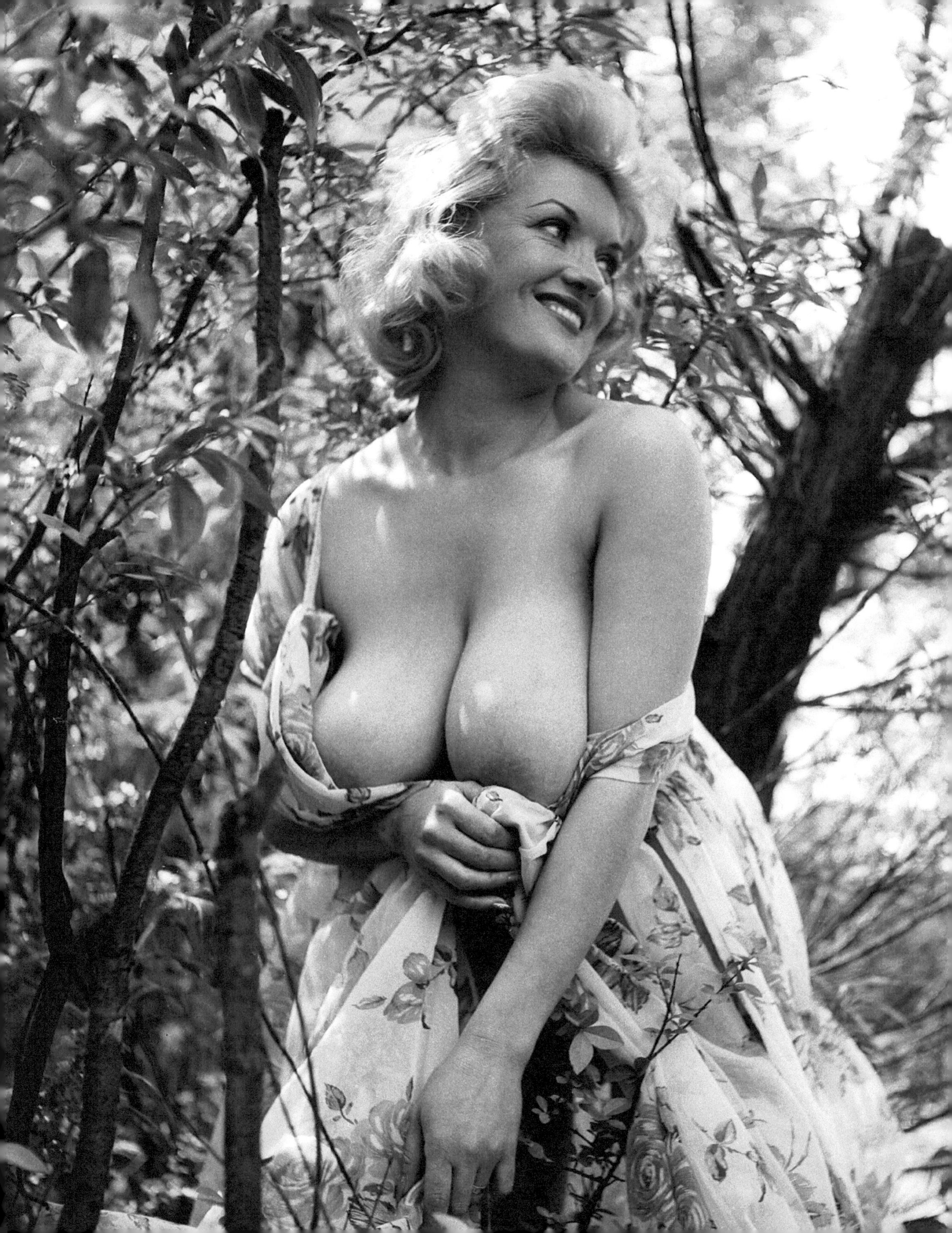

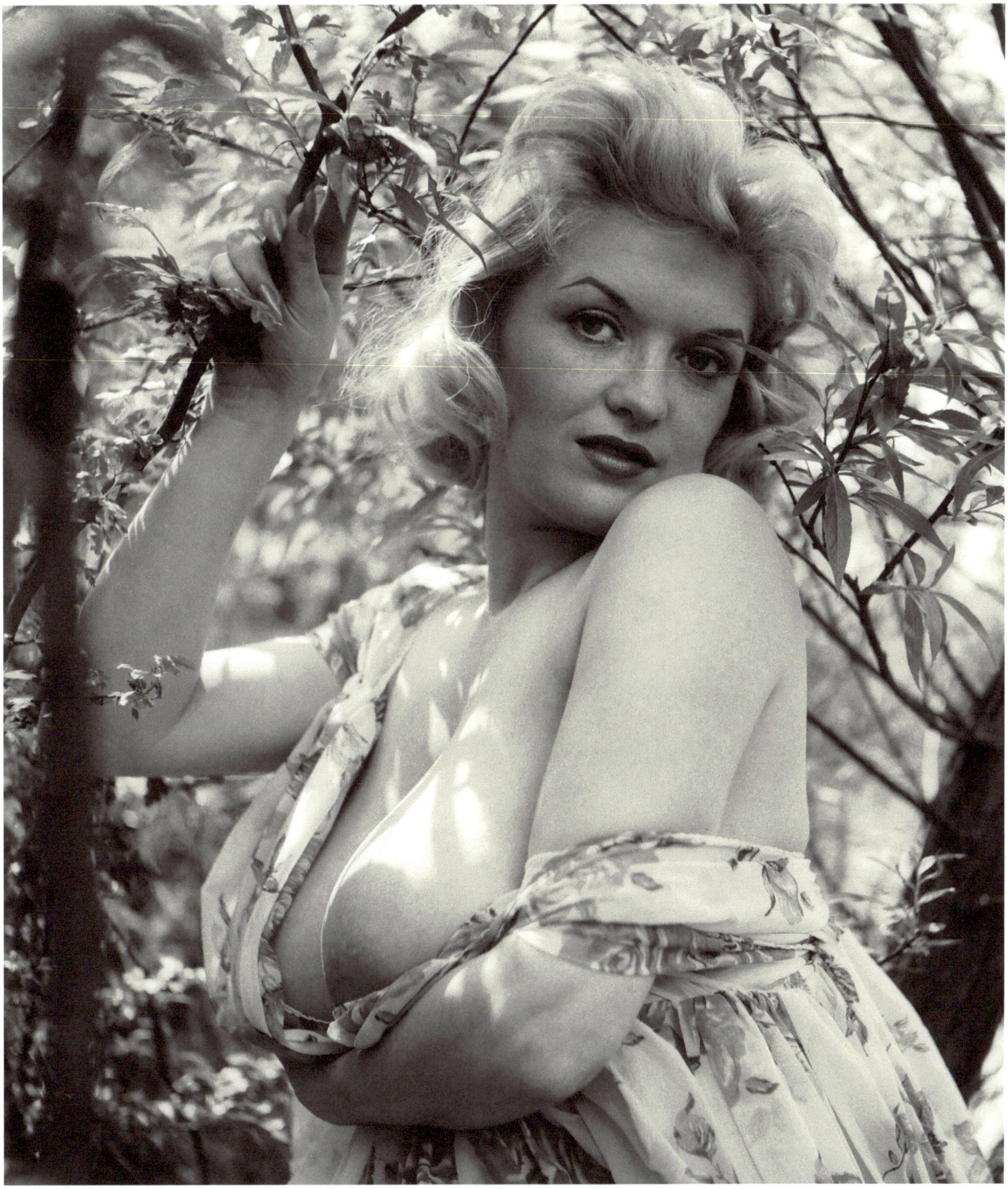

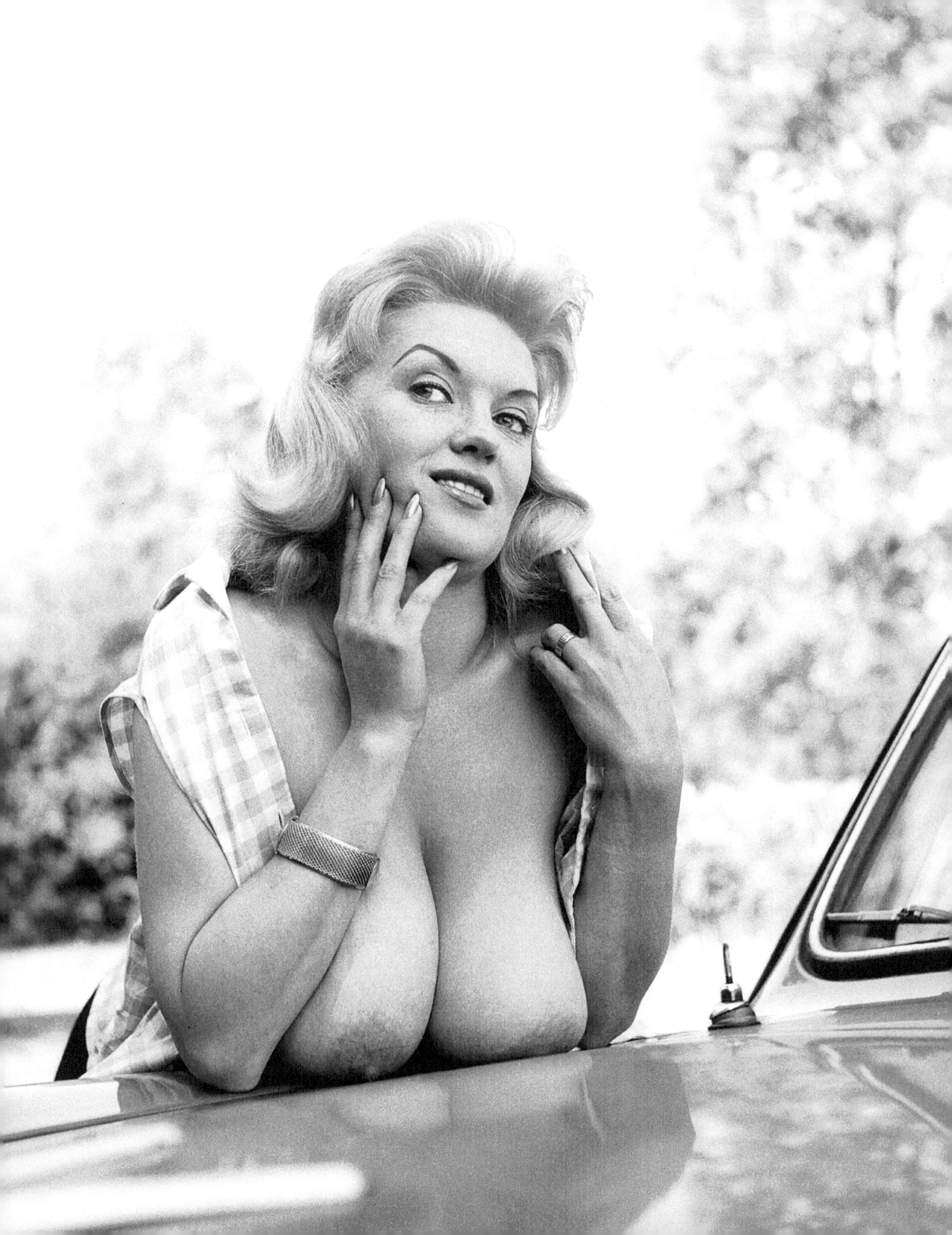

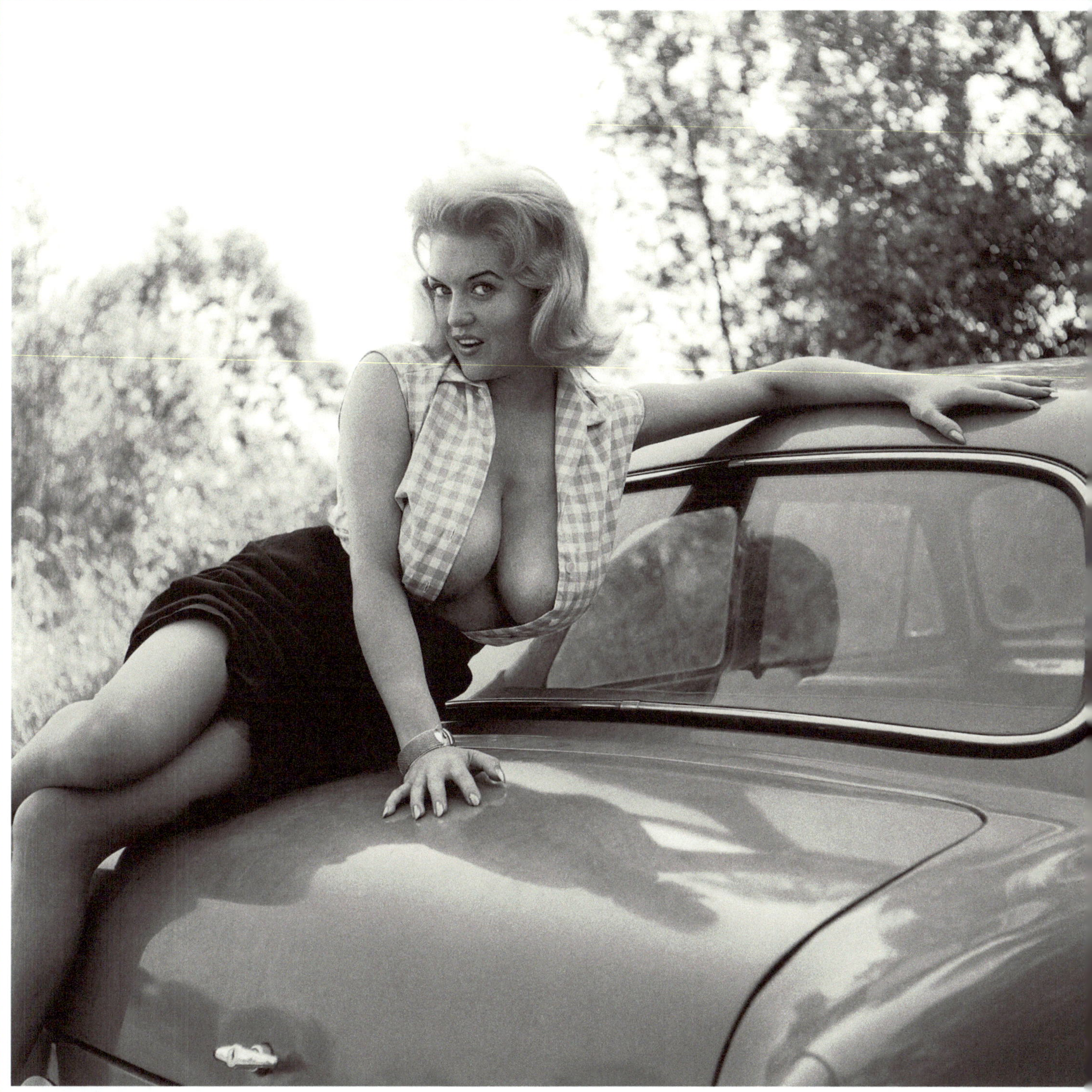

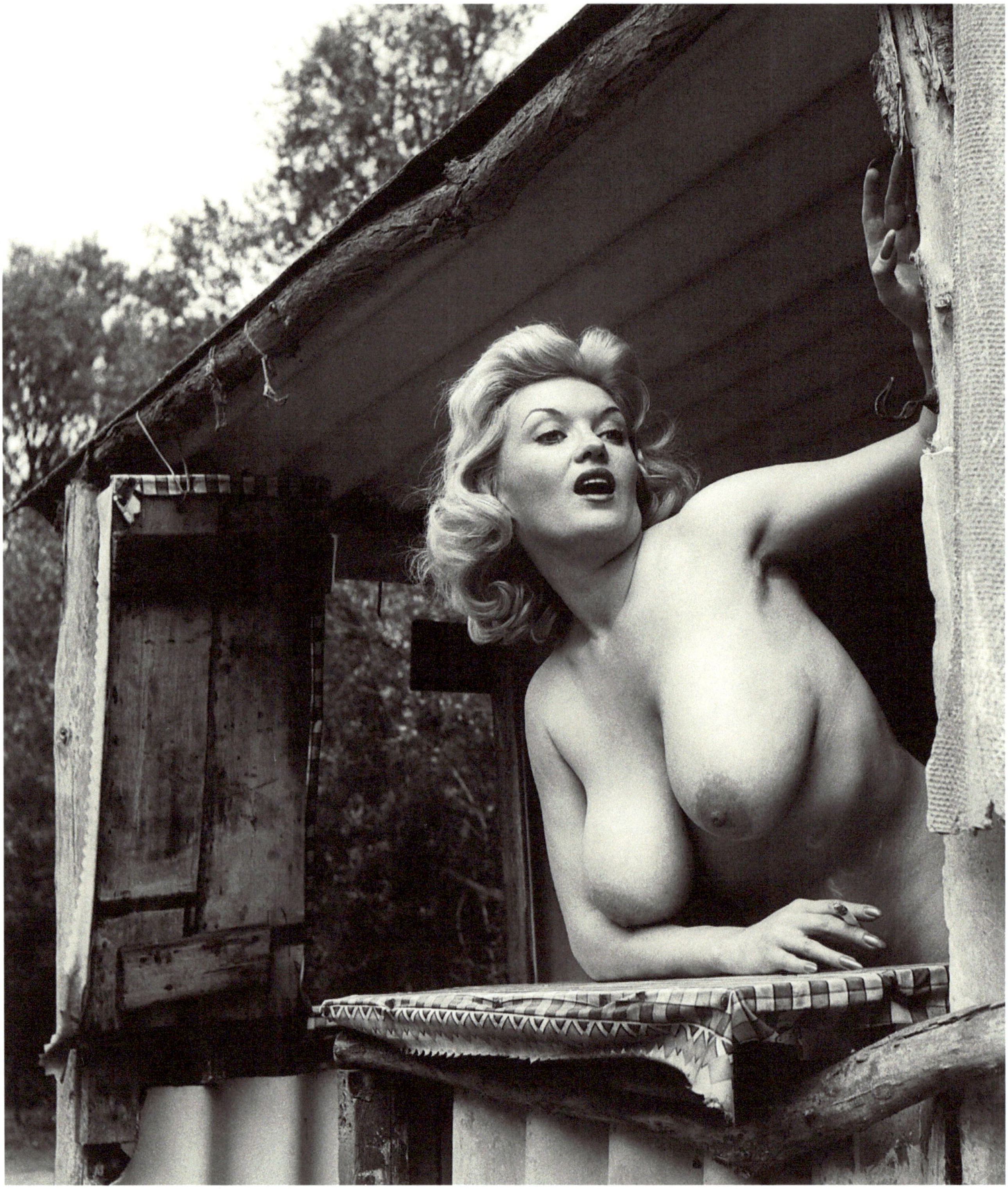

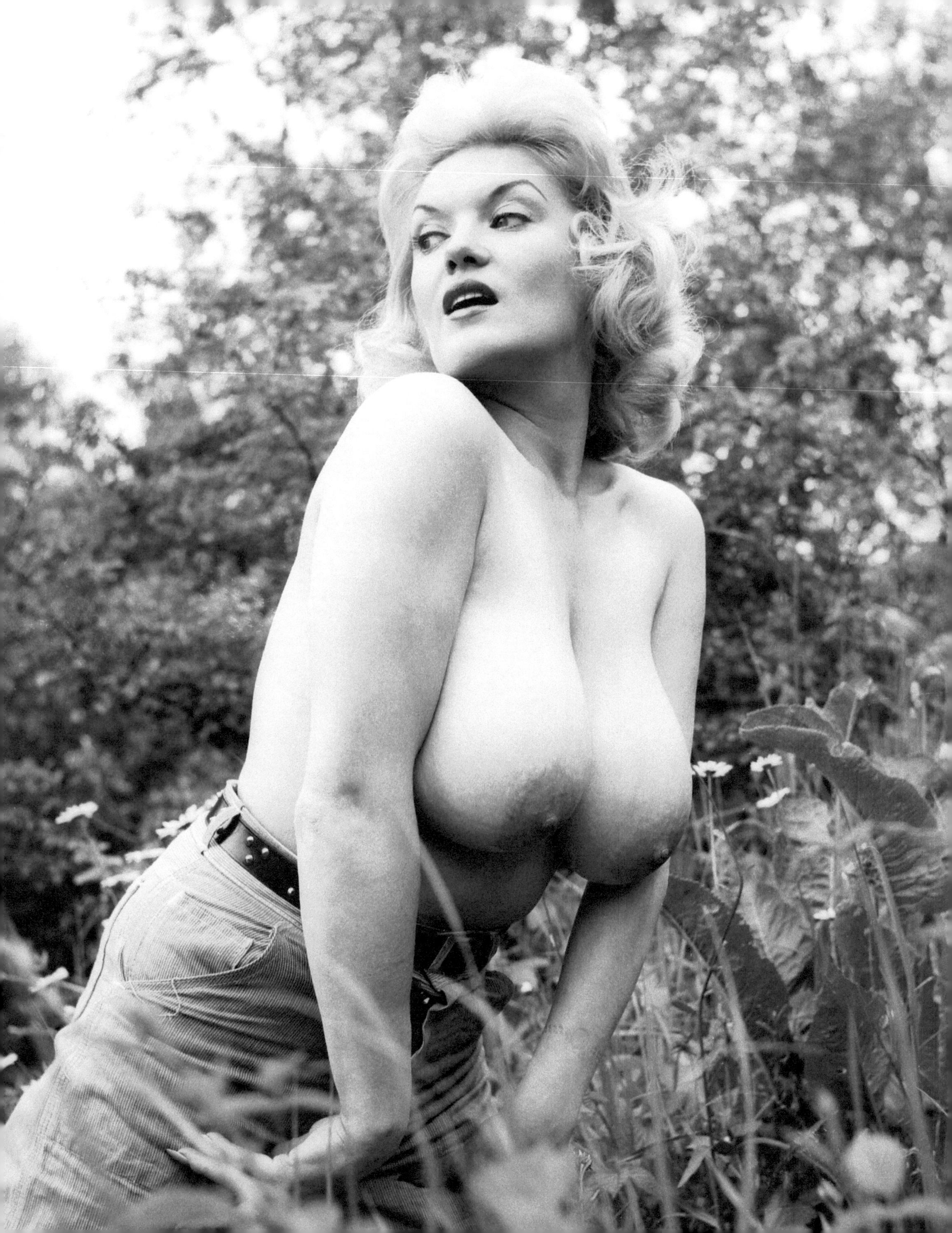

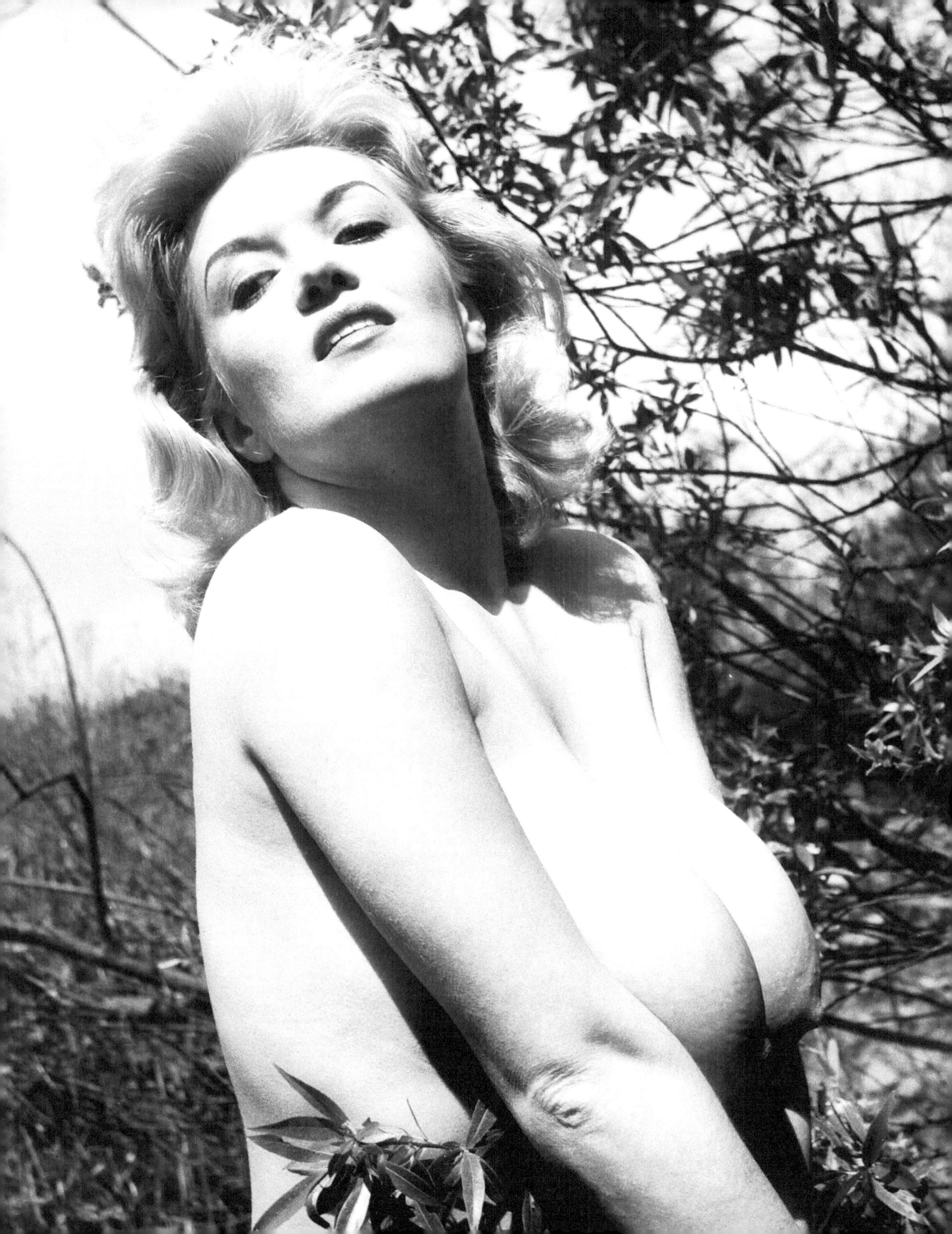

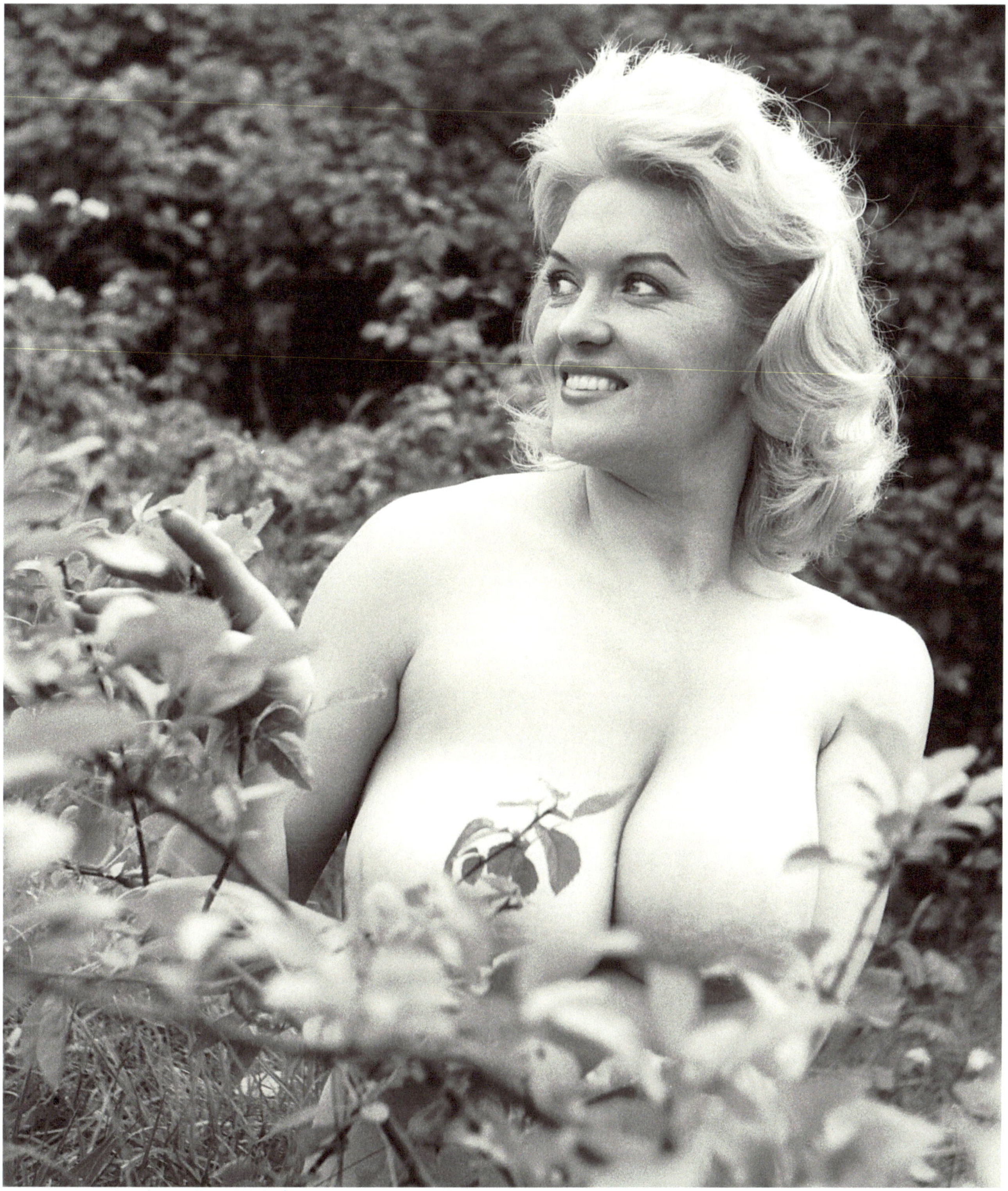

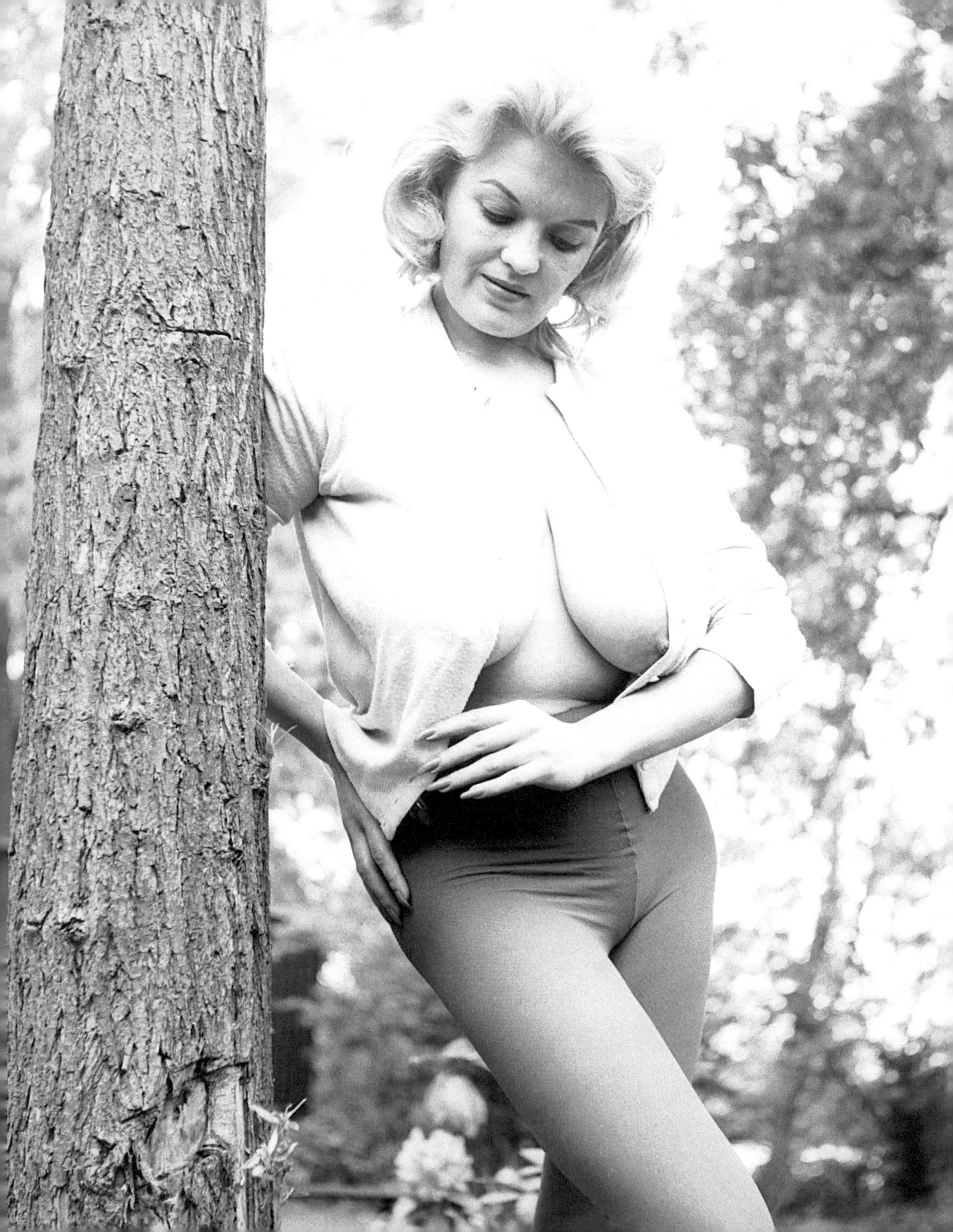

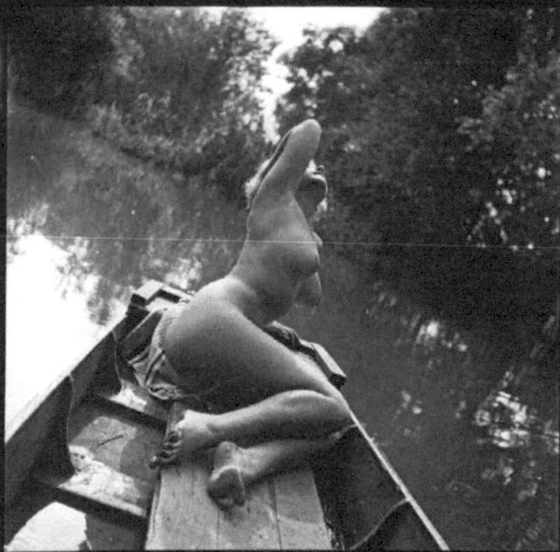
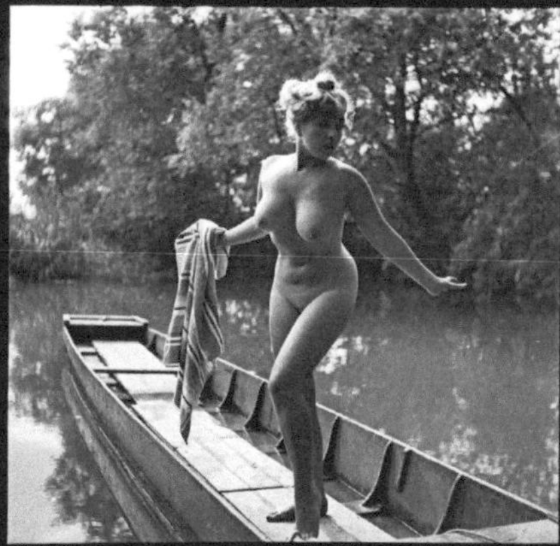
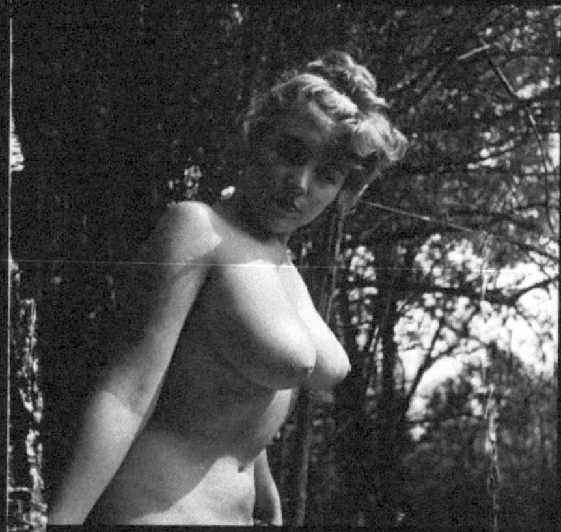
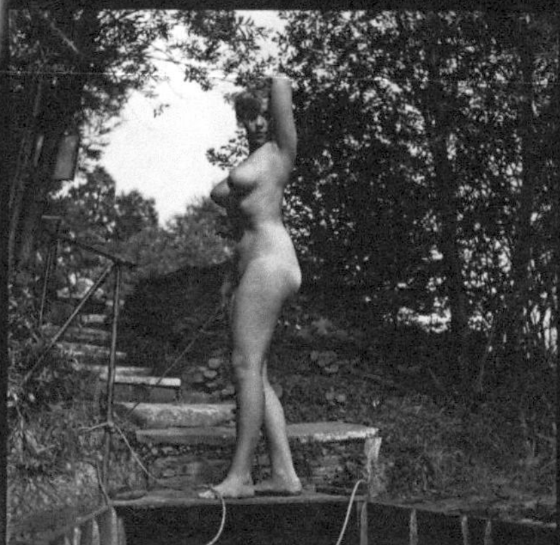

Tina Madison

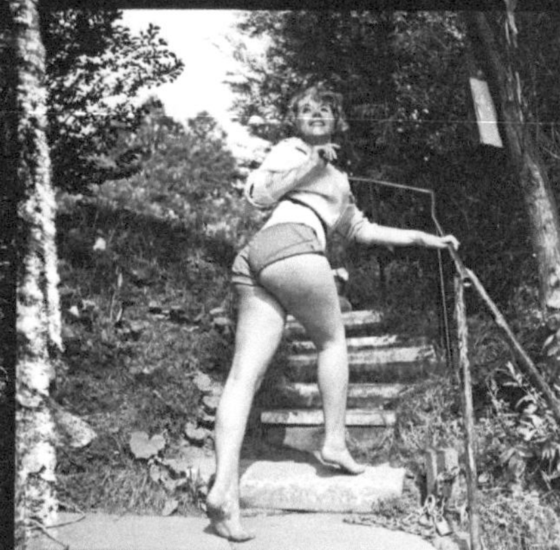
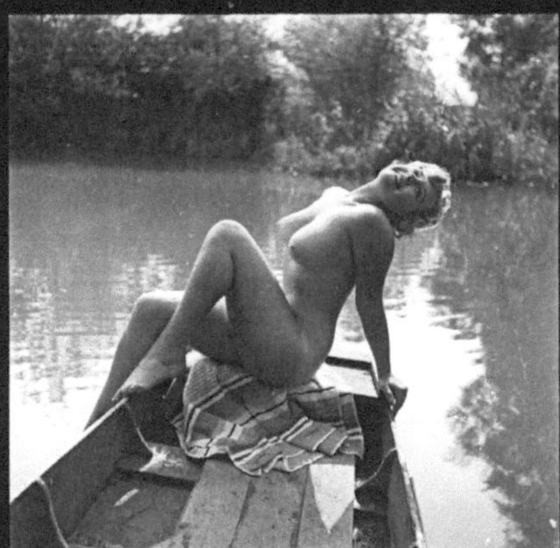
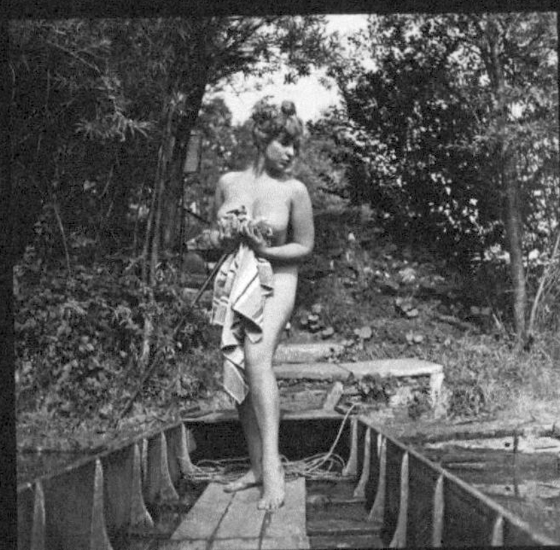
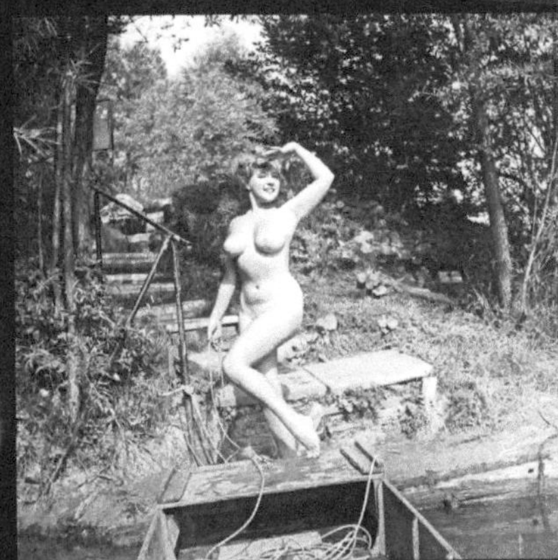
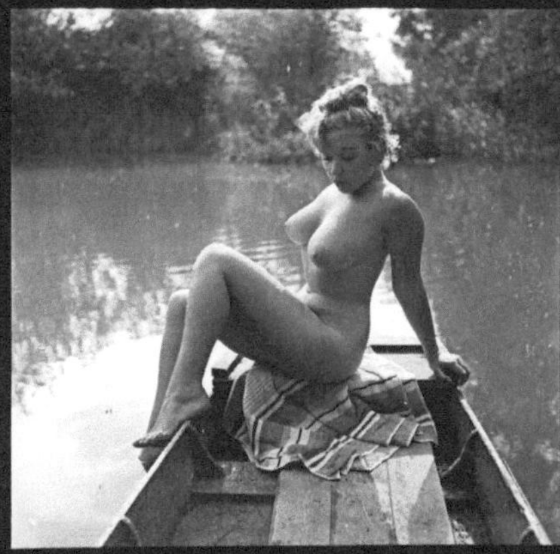
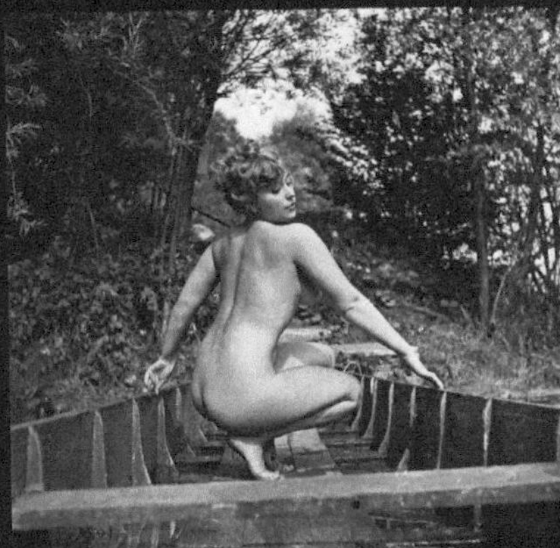
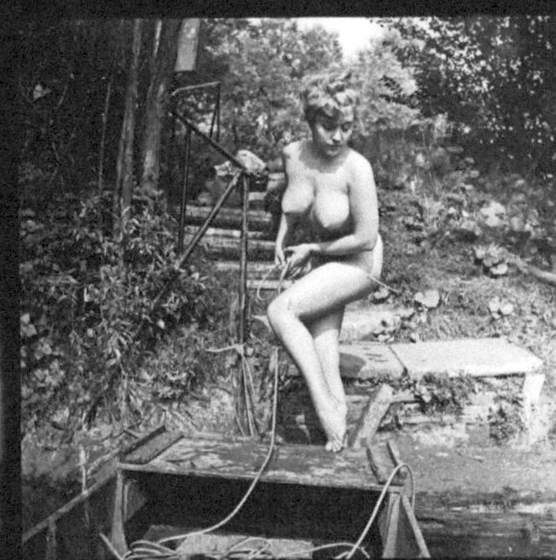

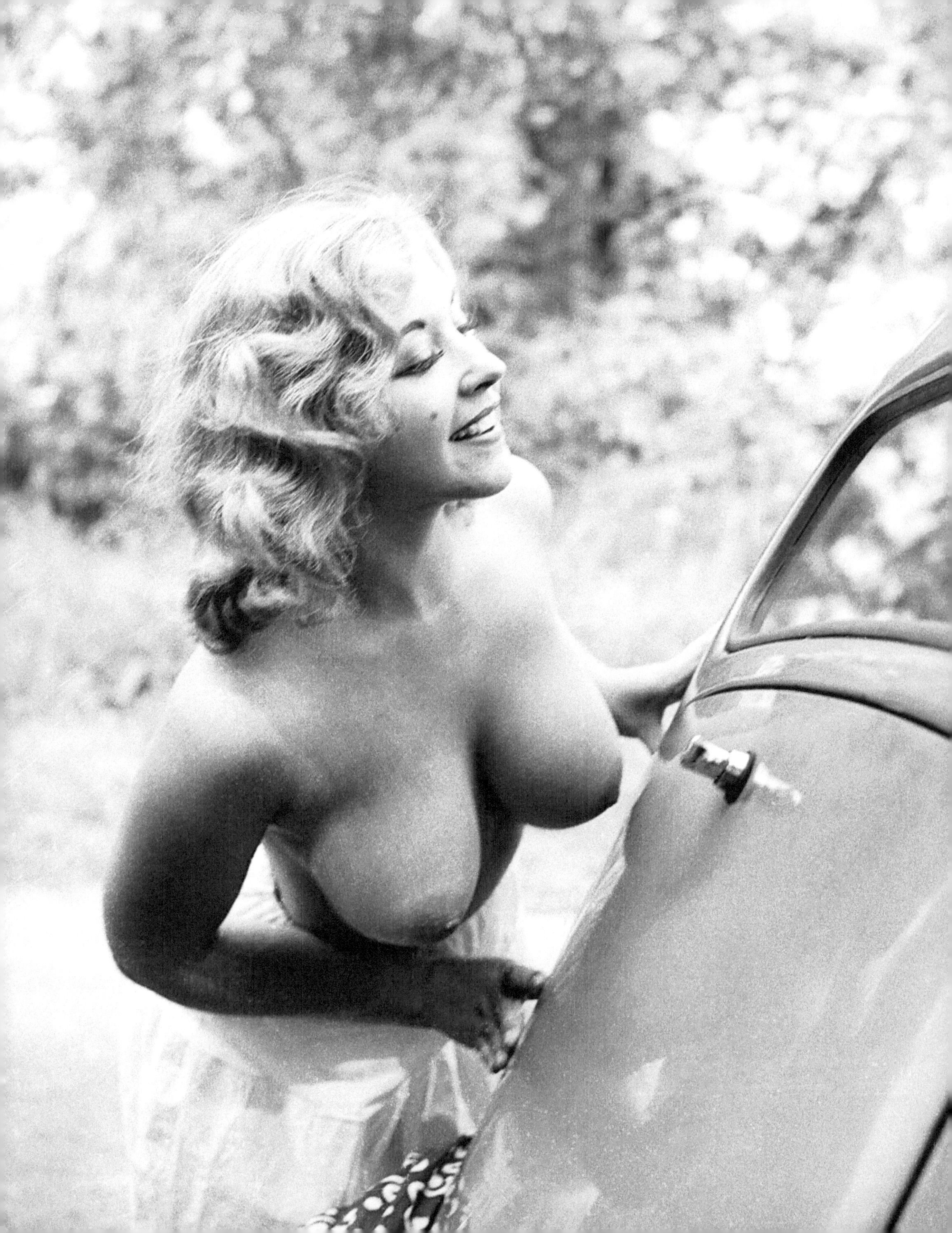

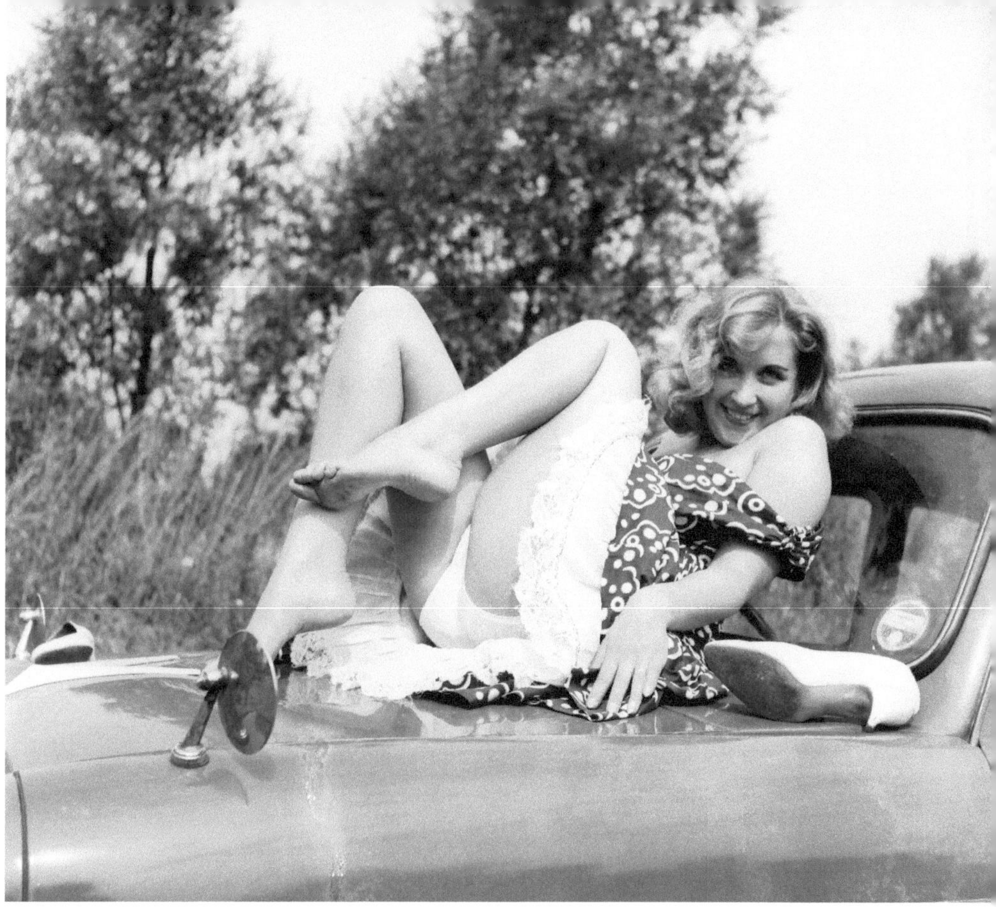
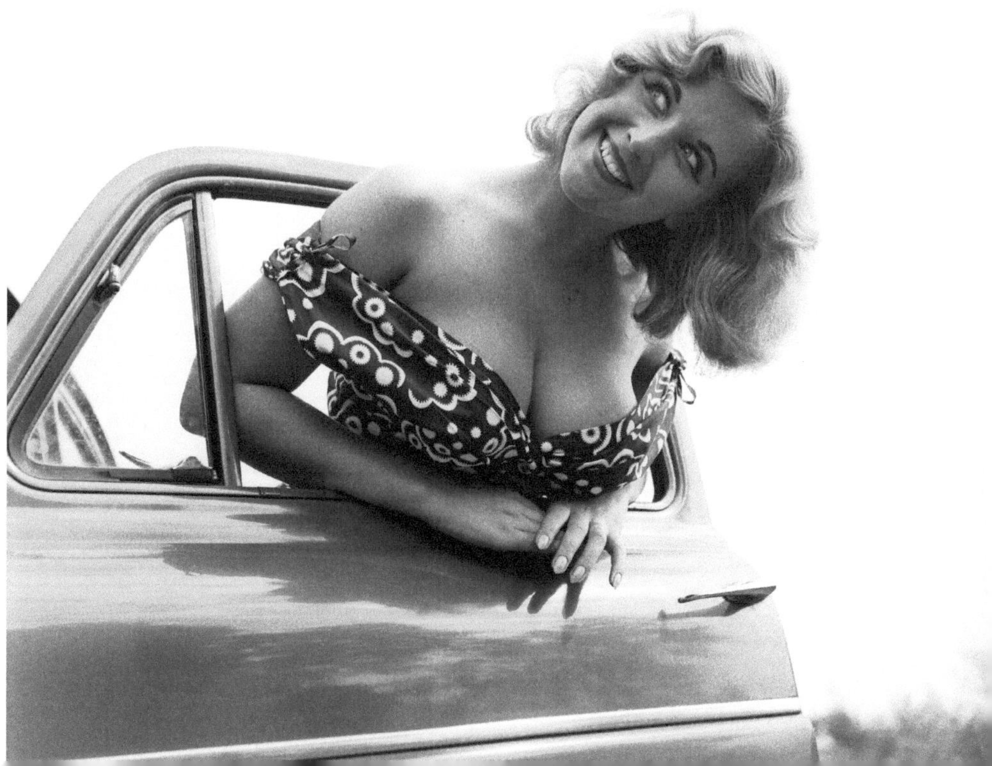

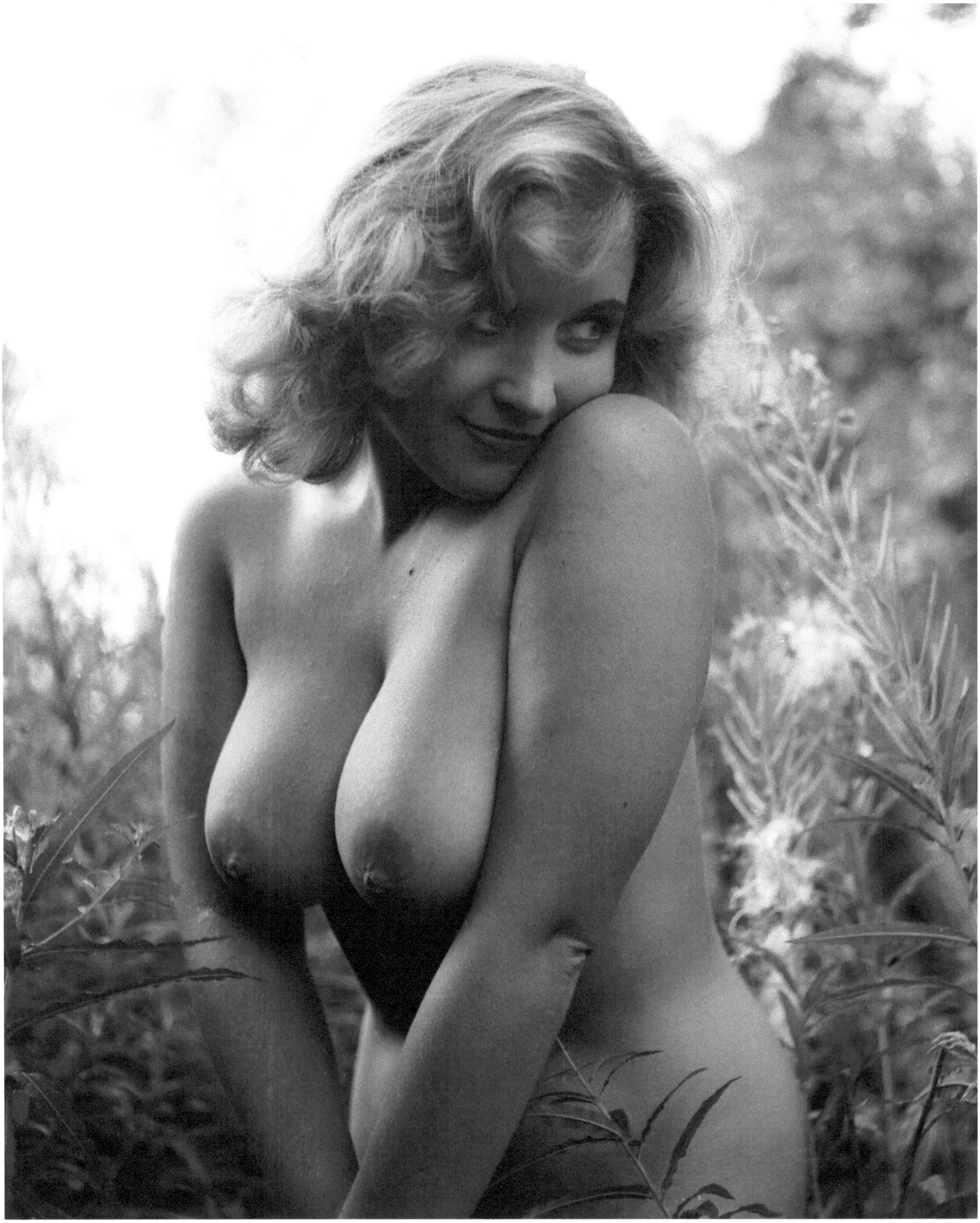

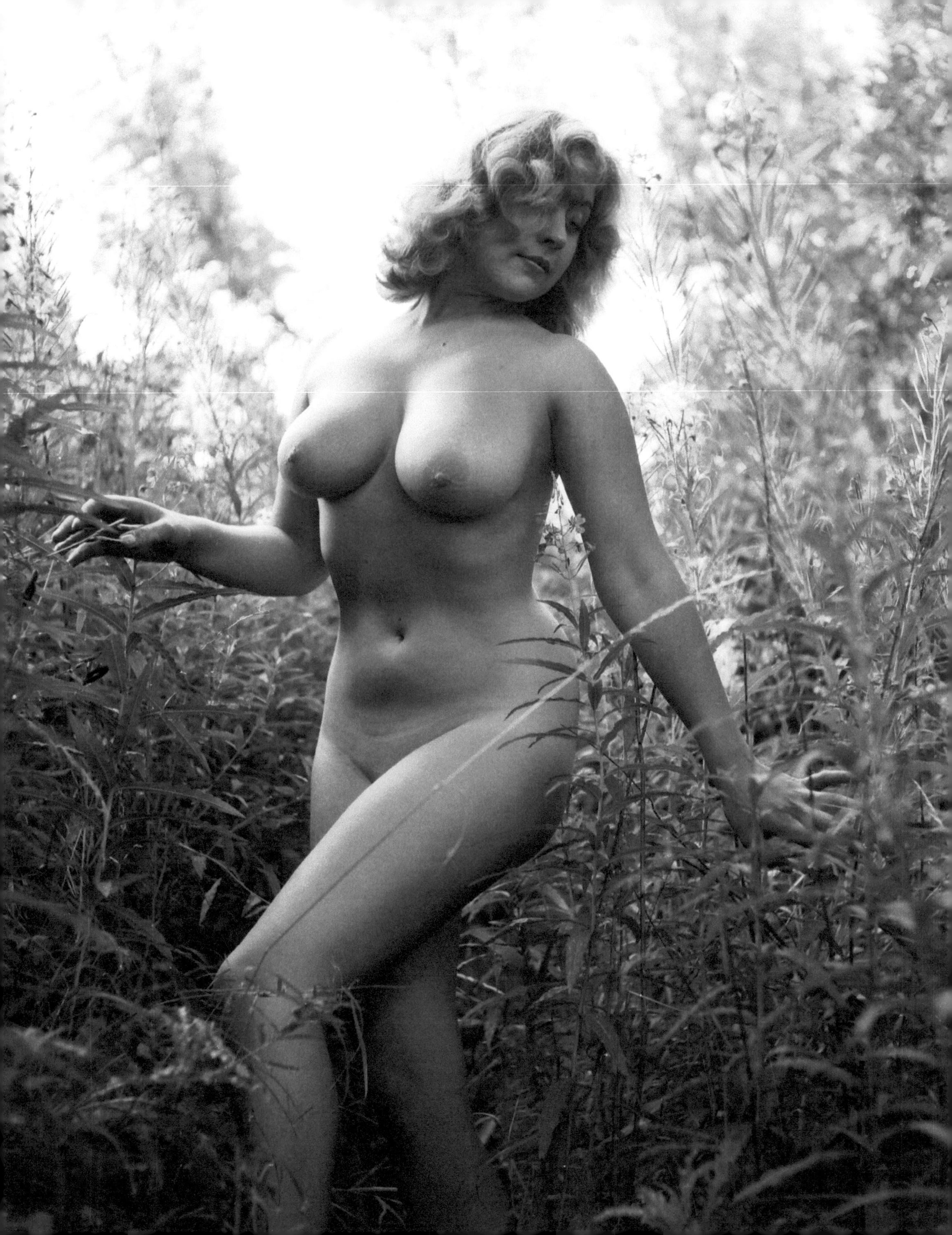

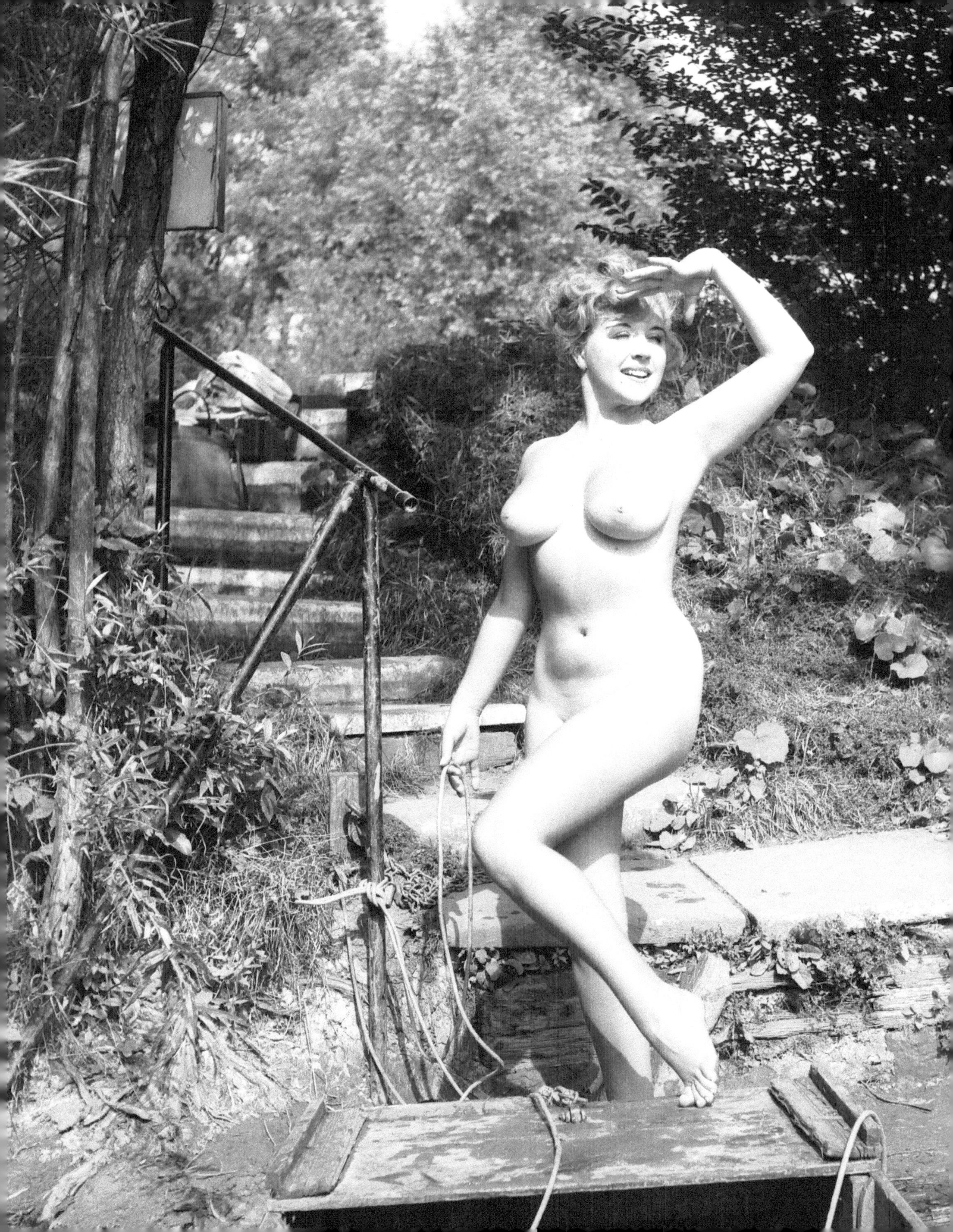

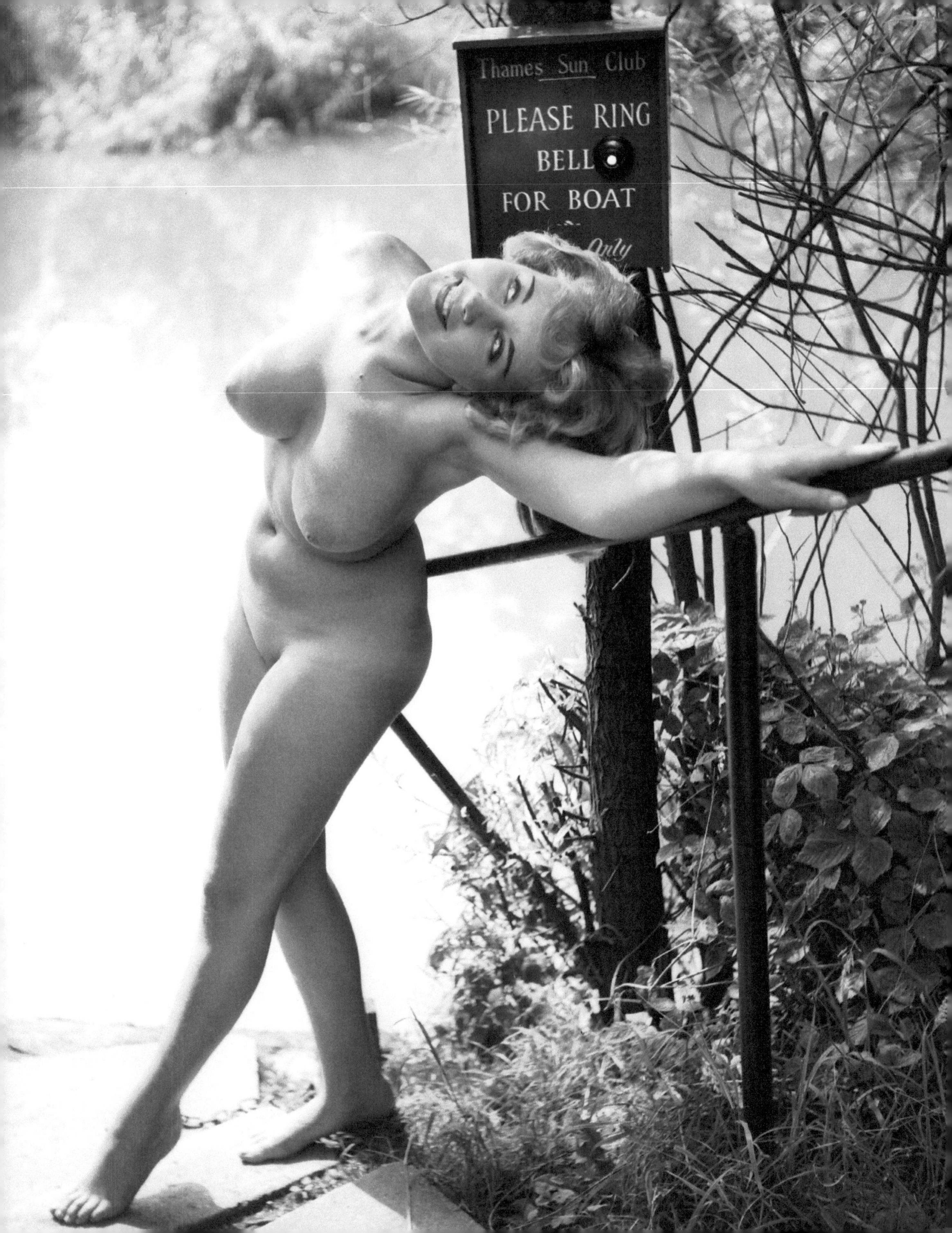
Thames Sun Club
PLEASE RING
BELL
FOR BOAT

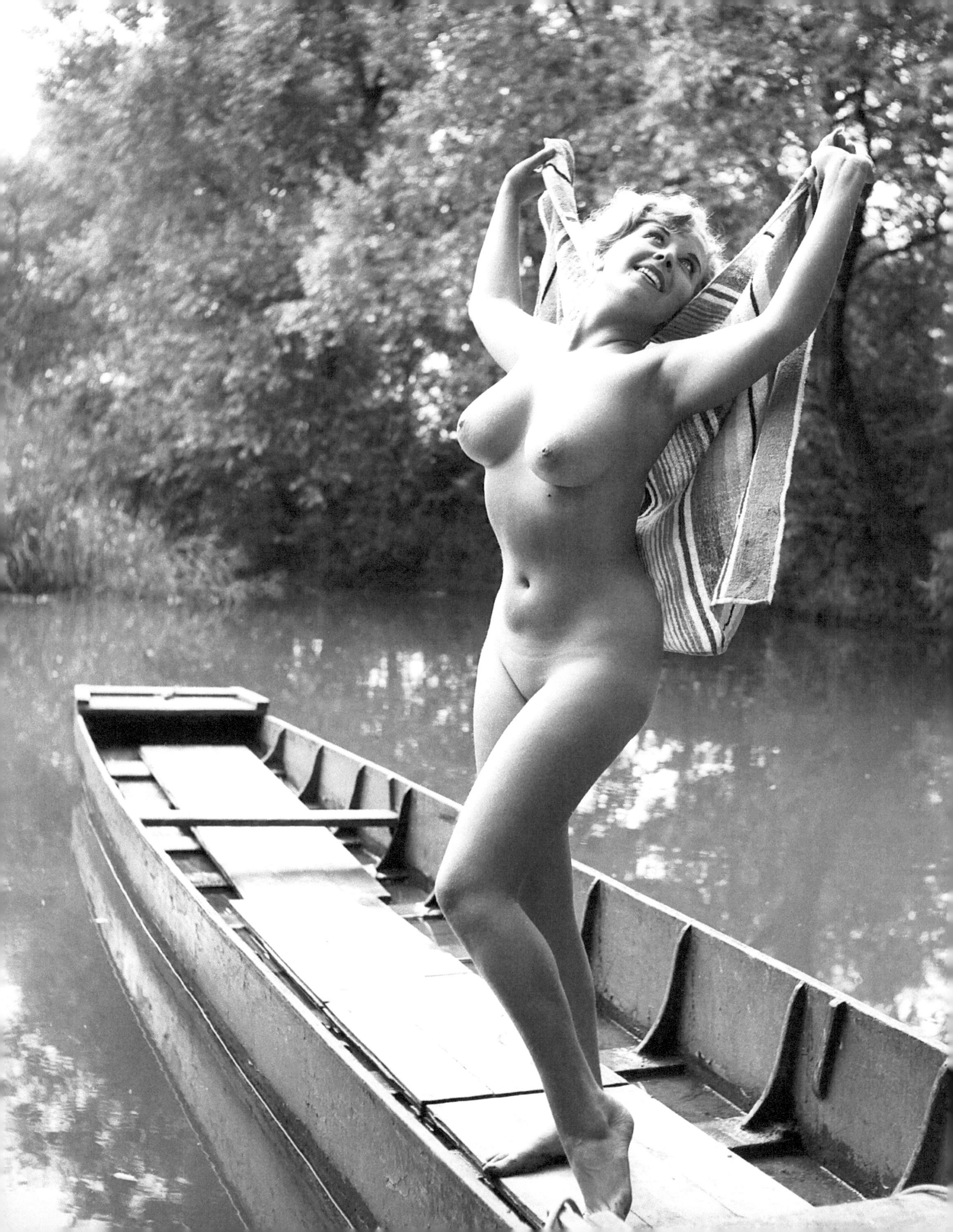

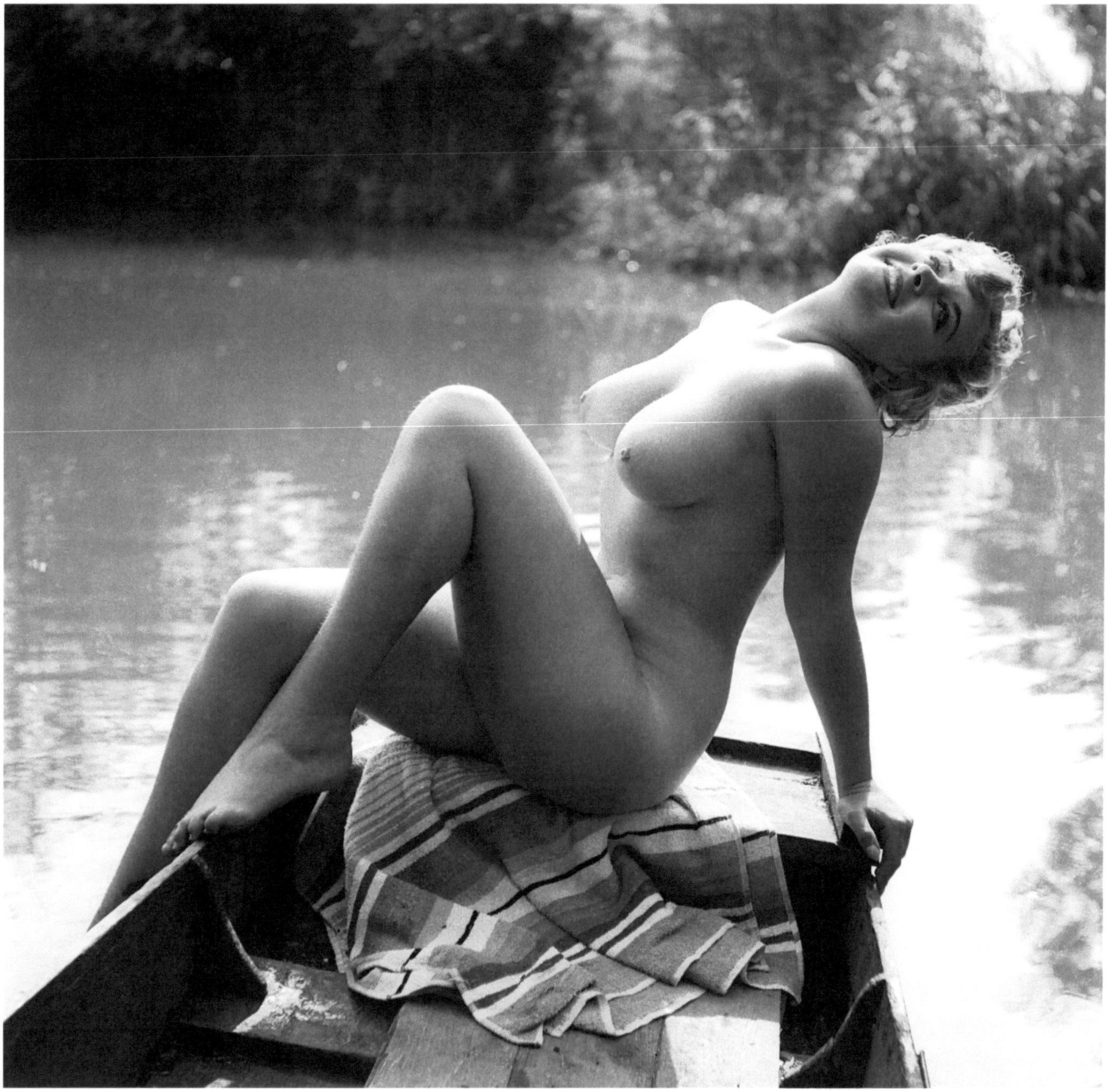

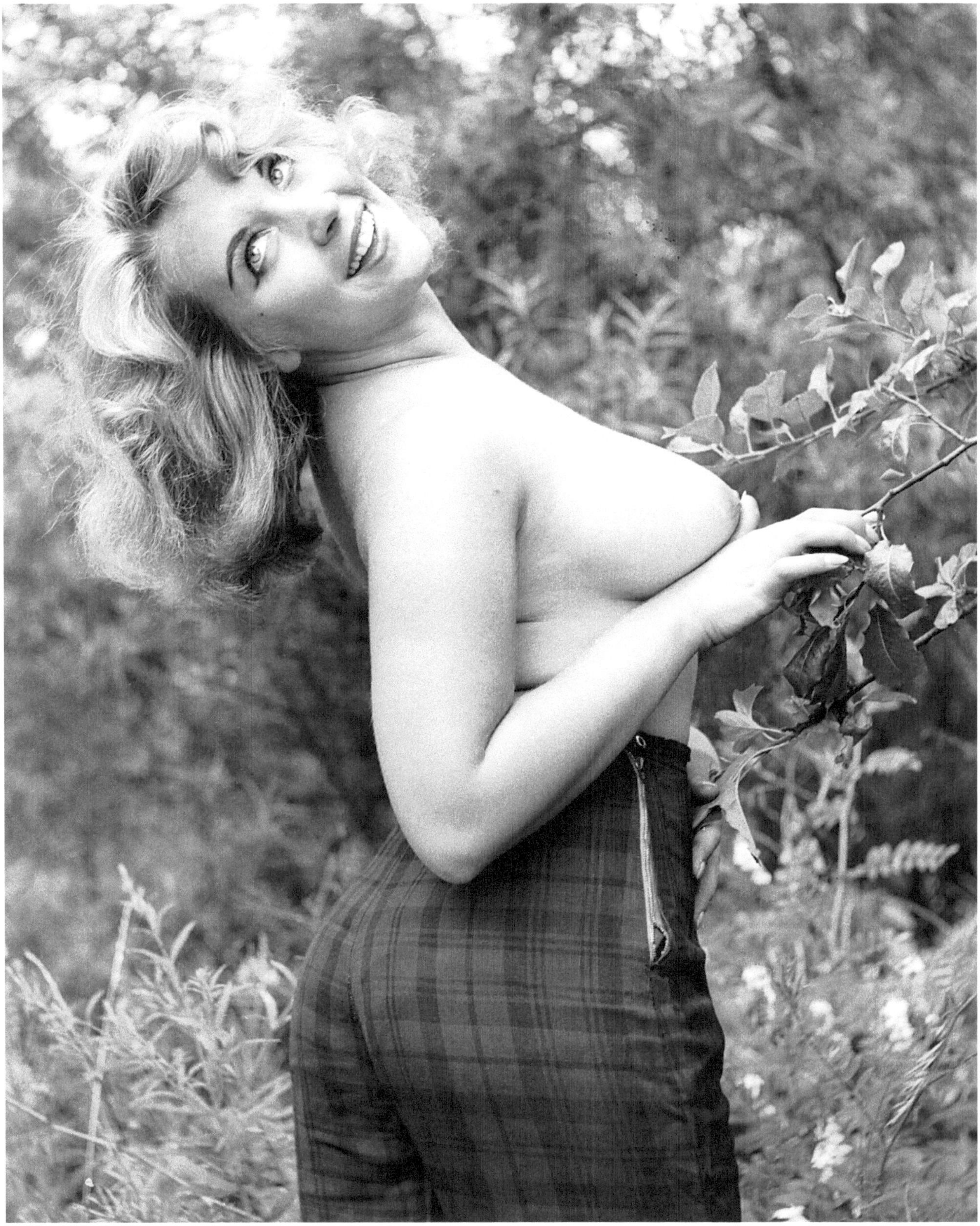

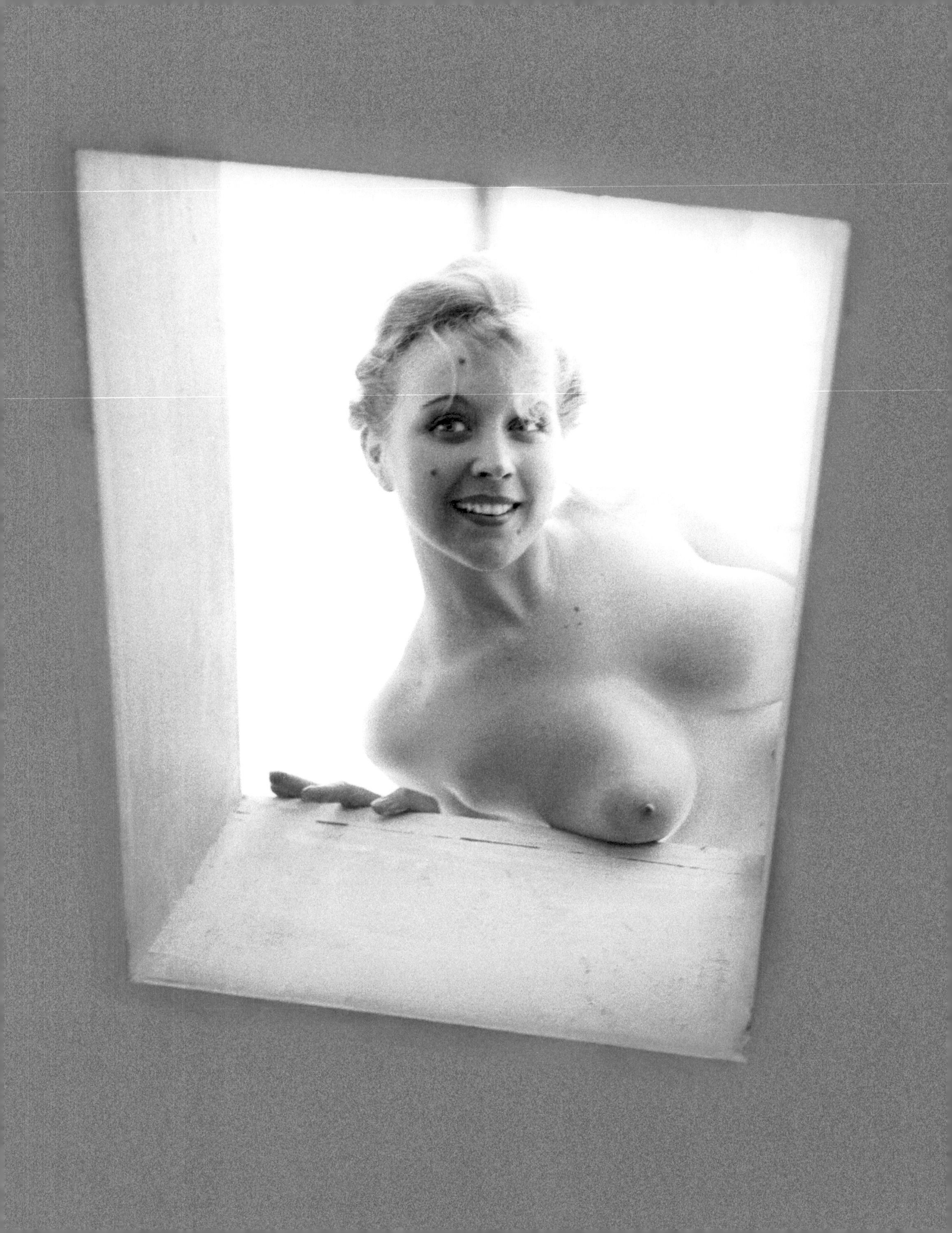

WOLFBAIT

UNDER THE COUNTER CULTURE

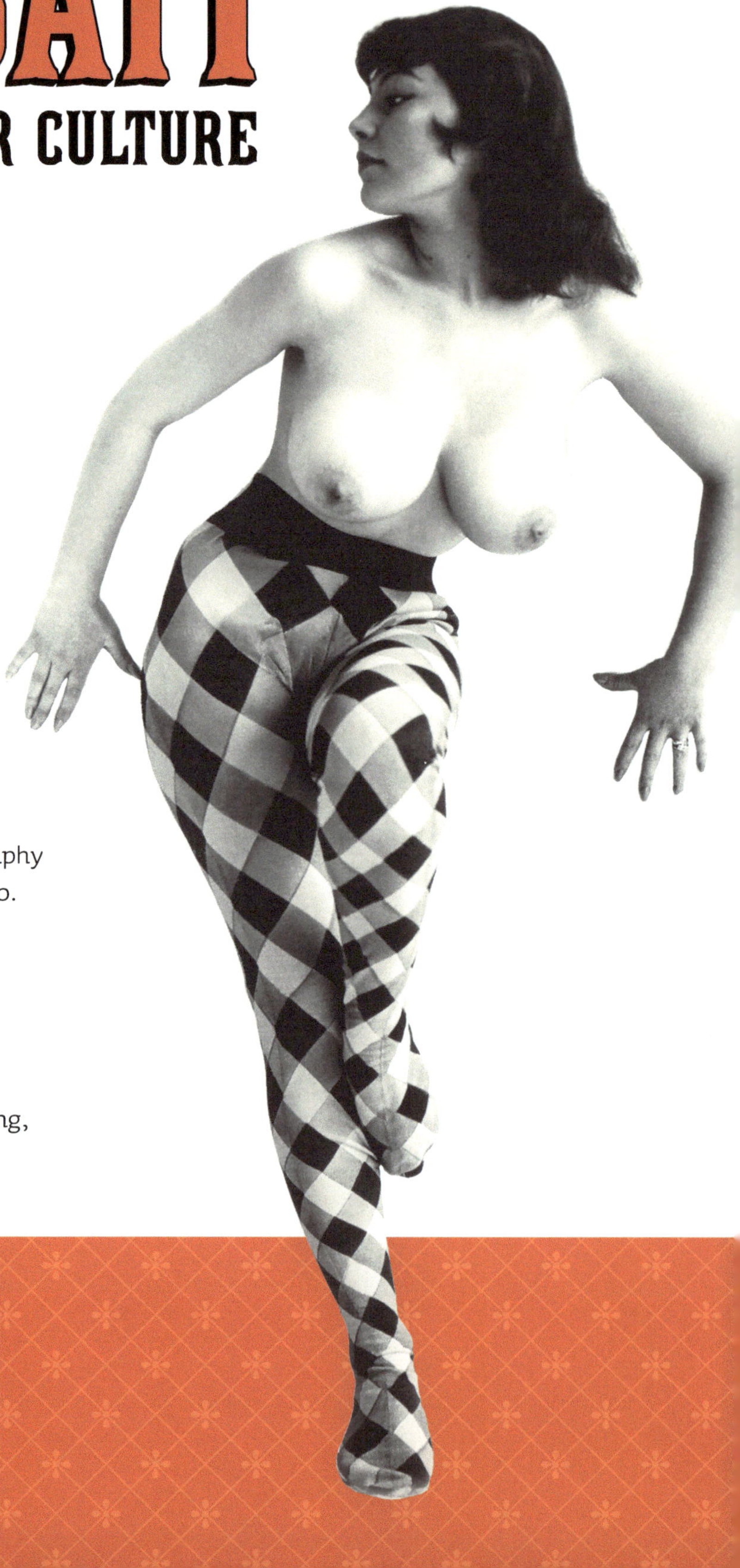

ALSO AVAILABLE

Cinema au Naturel
A history of nudist film.

Miniten: Rules of the Game
Invented in the 1930s, Miniten is a tennis-like game played by naturists.

Naked as Nature Intended
The epic tale of a nudist picture by Pamela Green, with photographs by Douglas "Dambuster" Webb, DFM.

The Naked Truth About Harrison Marks
The notorious biography by Franklyn Wood.

Past Masters of the Nude
An illustrated bibliography of nude photography books published in England from 1896 to 1960.

Slide Show
A luscious look at the photographic slides of Harrison Marks.

NEW! **X-ray Specs and Other Vintage Ads**
A unique treasure chest of vintage advertising, full of tease and prurient silliness.

Doing Rude Things

The history of the British sex film.

NEW!
The Glamour Camera of Eva Grant

A short biography of Eva Grant, one of the world's foremost female figure photographers of the 1950s and 1960s, accompanied by a selection of some of her most enticing work.

NEW!
Line and Form

A nostalgic review of Eva Grant's glamour magazine of the 1950s.

THE STEPHEN GLASS COLLECTION

Amazons of Yesteryear

A rare, action-packed collection of images of wrestling women of the 1940s and 1950s.

Beauty Off-Duty

Relaxed, everyday moments caught on camera.

Naked in the Menagerie

A playful look at Eve accompanied by her animal friends.

Nudist Camp Follies – volumes 1 and 2

An intimate look at the natural and free atmosphere in Sun Clubs.

Nymphs and Naiads

Beauty unadorned and outdoors.

Poise and Pose

A magnificent series of photographs of female beauty taken in the studio.

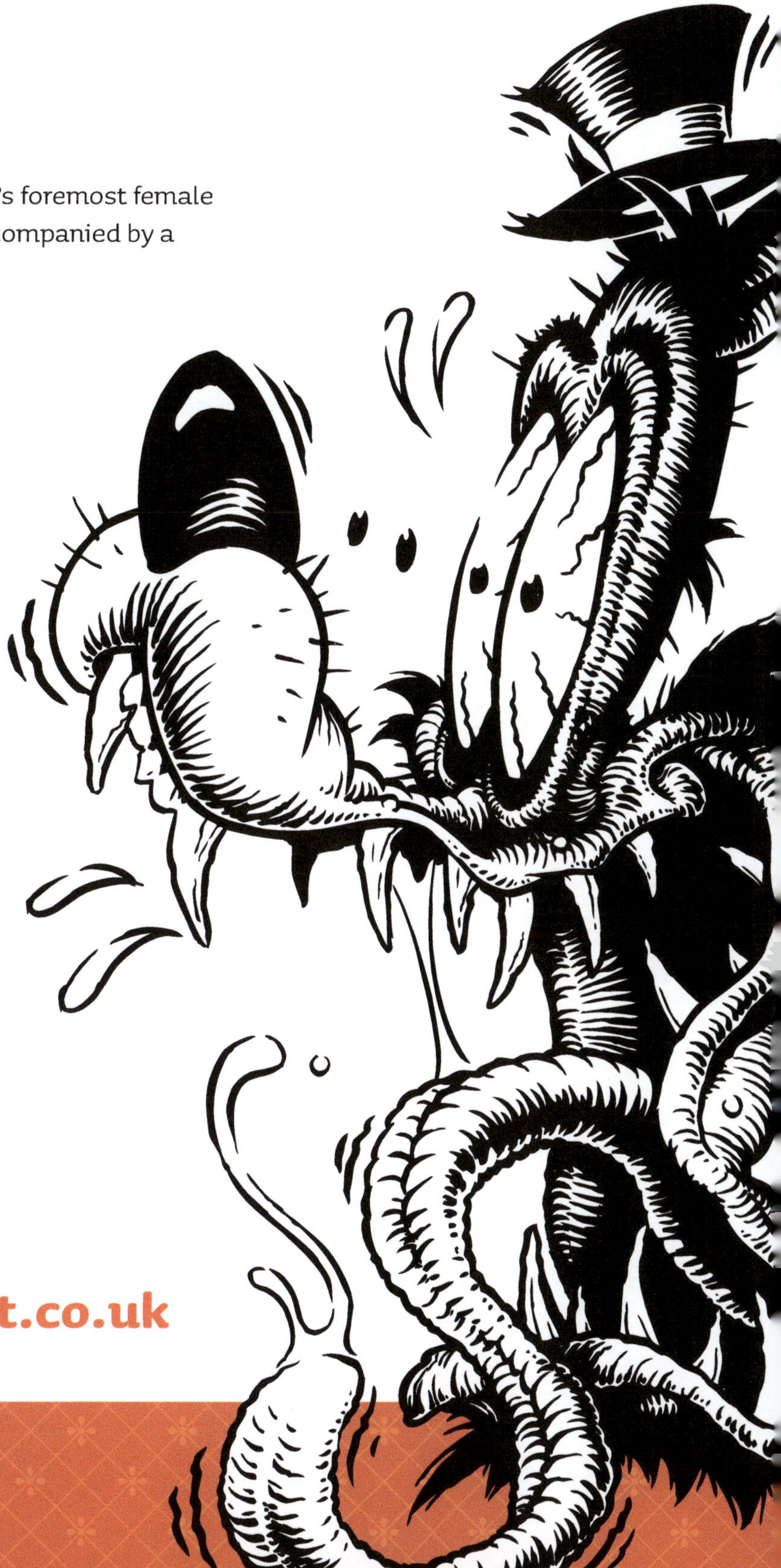

Order online at wolfbait.co.uk

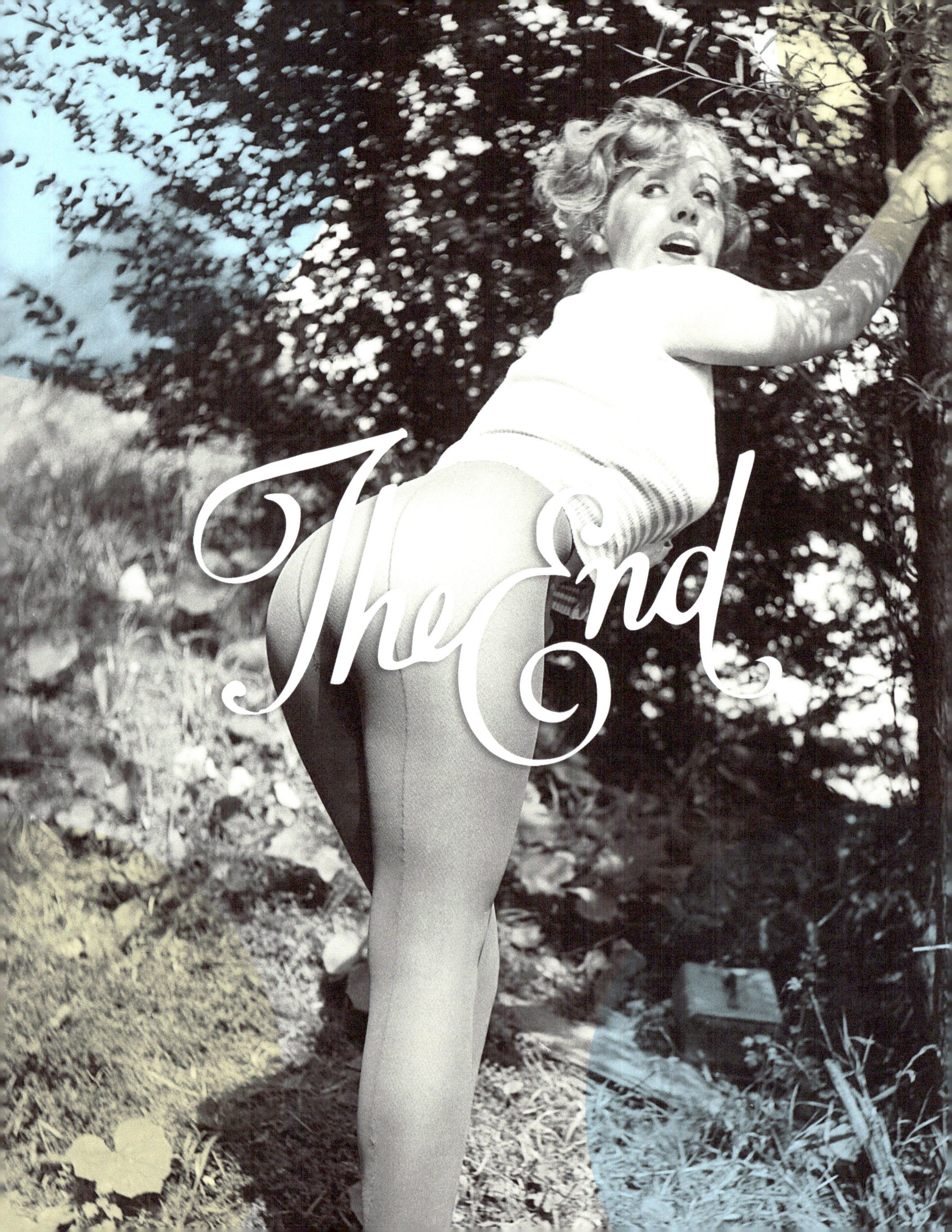
The End

www.ingramcontent.com/pod-product-compliance
Ingram Content Group UK Ltd.
Pitfield, Milton Keynes, MK11 3LW, UK
UKHW061034310726
14089UKWH00010B/231
9781916215191